A JOHN CATT PUBLICATION

T0273310

BE MORE TODDLER

A leadership education
from our little learners

EMMA TURNER

First published 2019

by John Catt Educational Ltd,
15 Riduna Park, Station Road,
Melton, Woodbridge IP12 1QT

Tel: +44 (0) 1394 389850
Fax: +44 (0) 1394 386893
Email: enquiries@johncatt.com
Website: www.johncatt.com

ISBN: 978 912906 72 7

Set and designed by John Catt Educational Limited

For F, L & H
I'm so proud to be your mummy

Praise for Be More Toddler

'This book is a must read for both aspiring and current school leaders and also trustees and governors. Emma manages to combine an incredibly engaging and entertaining style with important and practical messages, both for the profession and for the individuals within it. I wish I had been able to read it at a point when I turned my back on school leadership as the challenges of parenthood and the messy juggling this brings with it seemed too big a barrier. This wonderful book shows there is another way and that the skills and ways of thinking this chaos bring are actually helpful to being a great leader.'

Professor Samantha Twiselton OBE
Director of Sheffield Institute of Education (SIoE) and Vice President (External) Chartered College of Teaching

'In *Be More Toddler*, Emma strips back all of the leadership jargon and buzz words and she anchors leadership in the here and now, the day to day. Her honest voice, her down to earth attitude, her pragmatic approach make for a refreshing read. How many educational leadership books have you read by a woman? A mother? A flexible leader? A former co-headteacher? I will hazard a guess and say none. In a female heavy profession, we have a deficit of female leaders and a distinct lack of female voices being published. And Emma's voice is worth listening to, both in person, or in print. Written in digestible bitesize chunks, I can imagine teachers squeezing in a chapter between juggling their careers and their real life. Moreover, I have a vision of them listening to the audiobook whilst they are in the bath, on the treadmill or waiting at the school gate. I know that each reader will nod, smile and chuckle as I did as I read each anecdote. This book makes you realise that you can be a leader and be human, that you can be a leader and be imperfect, that you can be a leader and be your authentic self. Emma is a warm, kind and funny teacher/mother/leader/wife/human and she weaves the magic moments of bringing up children with the joys of being a teacher and a leader. She makes it clear that the impossible can be possible. Debunking the myth that you need to be a super hero to juggle it all and keep both your career and your children alive, she is my #womened shero, as she reminds us that it wasn't a cape, it was a dress, and probably a dress with a banana smear which is tucked into her pants as she mounts the jungle gym. "A leadership education from our little learners" is a must-read for all *big* learners.'

Hannah Wilson
Head of Secondary Teacher Training, University of Buckingham, former headteacher and co-founder of #WomenEd

'*Be More Toddler* offers a refreshing insight into the demanding, rewarding and important role of educational leadership. Emma writes from the heart, sharing her personal journey with readers in a lively, engaging and inspiring way. This book will have you nodding furiously in agreement, pausing for thought and laughing out loud as you are taken on a journey through the eyes of an educator with over 22 years experience within a plethora of leadership roles. *Be More Toddler* is the positive pep talk that we all need at times, reminding us of the magic, the wonder, the mystery and the creativity that both being a toddler and being an educational leader brings.'

Sarah Mullin
Author of *What they didn't teach me on my PGCE*

'Brace yourself, world of education: here's Emma. She's a gust of the freshest breeze in discussions around leadership. Far from the empty pomposity of much discussion in education, Emma 'gets it' – she understands that the apparently small things (the daily fabric of life and laughter and love) are actually what matters the most of all. Not only this, but that we have so much to learn from the very smallest members of society. This book is chock-full of gems which make us giggle, exclaim and have to dab at the corner of our eyes. Emma's is a wise and experienced voice, a eloquent and beautiful voice, and above all, an utterly authentic and unique voice that must be heard – and read – by all in education.'

Dr Emma Kell
Author of *How to Survive in Teaching*

'*Be More Toddler* is very much a call to arms. We are asked to change the narrative around leadership and even, heaven forbid, defy the statistics of the number of leaders leaving the education profession. Emma asks leaders to be as determined as a toddler, to hang on to your core purpose and be as focused on this as a toddler would, in spite of the mayhem around you. In particular, we are asked to keep the freshness and sense of freedom of a toddler, embracing newness in all its forms. This is truly 10% braver and Emma reminds us that we can be the leader we want to be. For me, the formula and the secret ingredients to brilliant leaders include delight and passion mixed with love. It couldn't be more toddler. I'm off to the ball pit – see you there.'

Vivienne Porritt
Education and leadership consultant and National Leader of WomenEd

Acknowledgements

There are many people to whom this book really belongs.

Firstly I would like to thank my husband, Tom, who has been my rock throughout all of the early years and chaos of raising our young family and who is never fazed by anything. He is quietly encouraging, utterly unflappable and just the best person to have around. Thank you for all the cups of tea, the laughs and for not being the slightest bit annoyed when I commandeered your new office in our long-awaited home extension.

Without the unswerving and unconditional support of my Mum and Dad, this book never would have made it out of my head and onto paper. Always cheerleading, always believing in me over the years through some truly horrible times, and some marvellously magical ones. I can state that I really did win the parental lottery. Thank you for everything you've done for me and for being the best nanny and granddad; you taught me everything I know about parenting and how all our children really need is love.

To my brother, Will, you may be the youngest but you're definitely the best brother. Thanks for always supporting me and for giving my head a wobble when I've been a bit of a div. Thanks for always being there to fix everything over the years from broken cupboards to broken hearts.

I would also like to thank the greatest woman in education and probably in life that I know. Thank you to my former colleague but friend for always, Claire Mitchell. There's not an edu or maternity or life storm we haven't weathered together and every day I have worked with you has been a complete joy. I'm honoured to call you my friend and this book simply wouldn't exist without all the things we did together. Thank you for always being there, for the laughs and the craziness and the fact that we just ruddy did it – Thelma and Louise, Tess and Claudia, Stormzy and Christina, Bert and Ernie 4 eva.

Thanks to all of team Latimer past and present. I worked with so many colleagues over the years who became amazing friends. Thanks for making work feel like a day with your bestest of buddies. The children, families and community of Latimer are so lucky to have you. #alwaysablue

To Paul, James and the DSAT team. Thank you for believing in me and for all the opportunities. I could never have predicted where this role would take me. Here's to more edu-adventures!

Finally, thank you to the three little ones who have turned my world upside down. Relatively late to parenting, I can say that it was definitely worth waiting for. I may not have slept a single night for over eight years but there is no greater joy than seeing you all smiling and loving life. May you always be as happy as you've made your dad and me. We love you so much and are so proud of you. Stay little, keep on wondering, have courage, work hard and be kind, always.

Contents

Foreword

By Richard Gerver

There is, I believe, a certain irony in life, that as children we want nothing more than to grow up and once we have, we lament our lost youth. Some years ago, I was working with a major tech company and the CEO was complaining that despite being able to appoint some of the best and the brightest, her team were frustratingly incapable of dealing with change, taking risks and self-leadership. A little glibly, I told her that she should only employ people under five years old.

I remember when I was training to be a teacher, one of my lecturers told us that we learn somewhere between 70 and 75% of everything we learn in our lifetime before we are five years old. I'm not sure how you can quantify it to that degree, but I am still struck by the sentiment, in fact, all these years later, I am convinced of it. Young children are amazing. They are simple, instinctive creatures who assimilate so much. Every single moment of their young lives is new, filled with change, risk and opportunity. Amazingly, there are very few one year olds going through therapy, because they can't cope with the uncertainty enveloping them.

I believe that one of the greatest curses of growing up is the very fact that we are expected to be 'grown up'! We are led to believe that the answers to life come from logic, maturity, careful thought and – dare I say it – complexity. We become so preoccupied with the expectations of others and the way they perceive us that we try so hard to be smarter; we latch on to complex words and phrases, we want to appear well read. We become obsessed with our own inadequacies, as a result we tend to live narrower and narrower lives, like an iris constricting the pupil in the eye as the light shines brighter. As a result, we stop trusting our own instincts that are forged by our own experiences, we doubt ourselves, double guess and reside in the 'better' and often more complex 'wisdom' of others – people who appear bigger, better and more grown up than us. As Eeyore would often say: 'Oh dear.'

I have long believed that a pursuit of simplicity is the key to almost everything and that the ability to regain the attitudes of childhood a powerful catalyst.

Be More Toddler is the book I wish I had written (*grrrrrr*), but I am prepared to overcome my own childish jealousy to celebrate what Emma has done here. I salute her bravery, her honesty, her extraordinary ability to strip down complexity in order to uncover deep and wonderful insights into leadership, life and learning. This is a book that takes the awe and wonder of childhood, the wisdom of experience and the joy of living and acknowledging life by identifying the simple stuff around us so that we can all find ways to solve the complex problems that challenge us every day. I urge you all to fill your anyway up cup with a glass of something sweet and fruity, settle down in a cushiony corner and revel in the joy of her simple 'childish' wisdom.

Section 1:
Setting the scene

Chapter 1: The ball pit revelation

Leadership needs to change. The way we look at leadership needs to change. The way we *talk* about leadership needs to change. For too long – despite the hundreds of leadership books and courses out there and their diverse formats, diagrams, styles, presenters and writers – they all had one generic central narrative. Be present, be clear, get results, and they definitely don't mention in them that you might also be trying to do all of that whilst juggling three children under five. When I was on maternity leave with my third baby in five years, I searched the internet for a voice which would help encourage me to see that leadership was doable, not just for me in my current situation (which was knee-deep in nappies and imposter syndrome) but for anyone who doubted that they could be a leader. Anyone who thought leadership was some mystical trait that you would either be born with or you would magically acquire in some kind of superhero twirl in a phone box, emerging with your cape flapping, hands on hips and staring down the future, ready to face the leadership challenges head on.

There are hundreds of potential leaders out there who think that leadership might not be for them; that they are somehow not like all the leaders they know or whose voices they hear in the leadership libraries but there is so much untapped skill and ambition out there. This book aims to share my learning from a multitude of leadership roles. From National Strategy consultant at age 26 to lead teacher roles, subject leader, assistant and deputy head roles in school, from my experience of working for eight years in one of the country's first all-female co-headships, through to working part-time as a research and CPD lead for a large multi-academy trust. I've worked in many leadership roles over the last 22 years and I'll let you into a secret too: I'm no superhero.

Juggling parenthood and leadership can mean that many leadership messages don't resonate: you end up sticking out rather like a sore thumb in the leadership world. But instead of viewing ourselves as sore thumbs, this book will hopefully help you to see that you really *can* do leadership. The narrative around leadership needs to change; we need to demystify some of its elements to encourage everyone to see they have the potential to think like a leader. This is not a 'how to be a leader' book – it's not full of extensive diagrams, multiple references to researched scholarly articles, nor does it profess to be a seminal work on effective leadership. What it could be though (and what I hope that it is) is a quiet call to arms for those of you who may feel they don't have the courage to think of themselves as a leader, or who just want to read something different about leadership. And that's another thing. You may read this and think that it is not at all about leadership and is instead all just common sense, but sadly common sense does not always translate into common action. Through reading about how our toddlers view the world, I hope that you see that leadership thinking really can be not only simplified but also explained very clearly, and often it's right there in front of us, grinning at us from the high chair and wearing spaghetti in their hair. Our toddlers may be small people but they are big on leadership.

Everyone has a story and everyone's story is unique. For everyone reading this they will have their own reasons for having picked up this particular book. I can only tell you my story but it is one that is echoed by thousands of people I have spoken to, both in real life and through connections on social media who have told me how they feel. They, for their own unique reasons, feel like leadership is somehow out of reach.

For some it may be that they are struggling to juggle caring commitments – be that parenting, caring for elderly relatives or a sick partner or child – for some it is other barriers due to experience, age, their own health concerns or because they are in another group or demographic which is currently underrepresented in leadership.

For others it may be that they don't perceive themselves to have the confidence or courage to think of themselves as leaders or the self-belief to think that they might well just do a rather splendid job of it. For everyone's reason, here is my story. I hope that, through the observations of our smallest colleagues, we all come to realise that leadership is not only doable, but genuinely appealing. May you all have your own ball pit revelation.

Chapter 2: Fading stardust

A ball pit at soft play may seem an unusual spot for an epiphany but that is where I had mine. I was amidst the migraine-inducing noise, primary colours, sticky surfaces and questionable smells of our local soft play with my then five year old, my two year old and newborn in tow, when I bumped into a former colleague. He had been an interim headteacher at the school where I had worked and was there with his brood of grandchildren. He was – as he had always been when we worked together – wonderfully buoyant, positive and hugely optimistic about not only education as a whole but what I had achieved so far as a leader.

During the conversation we reminisced over achievements and colleagues, and proudly introduced our respective progeny, and I found myself overwhelmingly happy to reconnect. My initial thought was to message my former co-head job share colleague and close friend to share the lovely news that I'd bumped into our old interim head. However, by the time I had wrestled the three tiny ones through the soft play security gate, convinced one of them that the woman behind the counter wasn't actually trying to chop her arm off but was just trying to attach an entry wristband, and then realised we had to all traipse back out again to change the newborn's ill-timed exploding nappy, I was exhausted and my colleague had gone. I sat in the ball pit, trying to balance a newborn and a phone at the same time to send that text, whilst wondering where my five year old had dashed off to and also ensuring my two year old didn't fall face first off the foam steps when, all of a sudden, I felt an unexpected wave of sadness.

I suddenly realised that the conversation with my former colleague had all been in the past tense. Everything he had referred to about me, using such lovely phrases such as, 'You were always going to do well, you had such talent' and 'You were a real star', were all in the past tense. It was as if all the bright talent and stardust that he had referred to had suddenly vanished and I was now a shadowy former version of myself. In the harsh, artificial light of the play centre, I realised my own leadership lights had somehow dimmed. At that point I had been in education for almost 18 years and I had worked tirelessly throughout that time to amass and share leadership experience alongside countless hours, weeks and years of extra study and work to hone my skills, but in that moment I was diminished. As I hauled my two year old from the edge of the steps by the waistband and set her on her feet again, I recognised for the first time the silent gradual erosion of my own leadership skills and presence. I realised that there was no one to grab me by my waistband and set me back on my leadership feet again.

In that moment I could so easily have become a statistic. The largest group of people to leave education after retirees are women aged 30 to 40 (37%). That is a staggering figure and whilst in that noisy ball pit, looking at my two daughters and my newborn son, I decided that group was not going to gain another member. I was going to defy the statistics. As I watched my middle daughter repeatedly try and fling herself off those steps I noticed the thin line of determination into which she'd set her mouth and the steely focus with which she'd attempt every jump. 'Now that is what I need to channel', I thought to myself, 'that toddler focus on getting things done and believing that nothing is impossible and that even if you fall flat on your face you get back up and have another go.'

In that moment, my idea of using observations of just what can be achieved by replicating the positive attitudes and behaviours of toddlers was born. My new three tiny 'colleagues' taught me more about leadership than any training I'd been on in decades and each lesson in this book will share a different aspect of this learning from these three most effective of little leaders.

Section 2:
Lessons from life's little leaders

Lesson one:
Setting the vision and sticking to it

1. Toddler leadership and developing leadership presence: Why the smallest chicks rule the roost

Have you ever walked into a house or a room or a restaurant, been there a while and not known there was a toddler in it?

No? Thought so.

Toddlers may be small in size but what they lack in height or physical stature they make up for in clear communication and presence. If you enter a home where a toddler lives, without words it's communicated fairly swiftly, and you know what this house is all about. It may be the clue of the pushchair in the hall, usually decorated with dangly books on stretchy strings or with its basket shoved full of snacks and other pacifying distractions. It may be the tiny shoes discarded in the porch, scuffed with hours of gleeful activity, or maybe it's the tinny sounds of children's TV tinkling from an open door, or the sight of a step stool leaning up against the sink of the downstairs bathroom. It's pretty much impossible to disguise the influence of a toddler in a home and should you chance to venture into every corner of every room you are likely to find further evidence of the toddler's adventures. This physical evidence is just the start of the trail of their influence. Household schedules are adapted to accommodate the new arrival and evenings now signal a wrestle through the noisy tsunami that is bathtime and bedtime, whereas previously it may have been a relaxing drink, an evening at a restaurant or a gym session. The 'work' of having a toddler, therefore, manages to instigate a change in everything from the physical organisation and furniture within the home to the scheduling of activities and changing of long-established behavioural habits. But how do they do this? How do they do this with minimal language, often-unsavoury table manners and anti-social toilet habits?

It's all about the triple buy-in. Parents have three drivers towards their children:

1. **They have the moral duty of caring for their child.** Despite the multiple get ups in the night, the upturned bowl of yoghurt on the head, and the third tantrum of the day about why it's not appropriate to wear Wellington boots and a snowsuit in a heatwave, no parent wants to be that one who simply throws up their hands and says: 'To hell with this; I'm off out. You look after yourself kid – I need a break, a coffee, probably a large piece of cake and a nap so I'll see you around lunchtime.' We can see the headlines unfolding about our poor parenting choices on virtual newspapers and we simply know that what needs to be done is the 'right' thing to do so we get up in the night (every night, oh yes, every single night), we clean up the yoghurt and we negotiate a way out of the snowsuit and Wellingtons without bolting out of the door leaving them home alone and diving into an Americano.

2. **The second is that we are driven by a love of what we do.** Despite the often seemingly unending treadmill of the preparation of miniature meals, changing of nappies and endless renditions of 'Wind the Bobbin Up' we still delight in the achievements of our toddlers and feel that familiar mix of pride and pure joy when they master a new skill or simply throw their arms around us and smile.

We are emotionally invested in the work that we do as a parent and reap real emotional dividends ourselves when our toddlers achieve or defy and exceed our expectations.

3. **The last is that we have a clear plan of what needs to be done in order for them to be successful.** Everything from the all too often elusive, 'sleeping through the night' to the more practical things of using a spoon correctly or putting on a shoe (on the other foot, the other one – no not that one, the other one!) are understood as key milestones by everyone who knows the toddler and are encouraged and worked towards every day. And, just as we knew that expecting a newborn to put on a shoe would be unrealistic, we are also clear that as a toddler, their challenges should be stretching but ultimately achievable. We are clear about the goals and the small milestones that we need to get them there and which we can celebrate, and we have adapted our environment, our homes and our behaviour in order to help them succeed. We have an often unspoken, yet still shared understanding with our friends and family too, of what constitutes appropriate challenges for our toddler and what they still need to do in order to continue to be successful.

In essence, we have three keys to setting the scene to be a successful leader:

1. **Moral purpose**: doing the 'right' thing.
2. **Emotional buy-in**: everyone taking pride in and enjoying their work, however challenging it may be.
3. **A clear, shared and well-understood plan** of action for improvement.

And, we have three key aspects of evidence we can look for to check if we're having an impact:

1. **You can see it**

   Is our vision or the work of our organisation clearly visible upon arrival? Is there evidence of the type of work we do, what we stand for and what we believe as soon as you arrive? Can you tell what we're about at first glance? Is there evidence of the work you saw upon arrival across every 'room' in our organisation?

2. You can feel it

As you watch people work in the organisation, do they appear happy? Are they motivated? Do their words and actions mirror working towards a common goal and is there synchronicity between different people or departments? Are they keen to talk about the success and the positive aspects of their work?

3. You can hear it

You can hear people talking about the work needing to be done with positive regard. There is clarity and purpose to actions and conversations, suggestions are shared without fear and constructive feedback is welcomed. There is a shared understanding of what is trying to be achieved and exchanges are purposeful and focused on improvement. There is a lack of negative conversation, intimidation or ridicule. The destination is set and everyone's attitude and conversation is geared towards success as a collective.

So despite our toddlers being the smallest chicks in the coop, they exert the biggest influence because they tap into our three drivers. Leadership doesn't have to be about being the showiest, the cleverest at everything (remember most of our toddlers have yet to master understanding of how a spoon functions), the loudest, or the biggest crowing cockerel in the yard; it's about buy-in and consistency. Creating a culture where, even when things are tough and exhausting, there is still a clear and shared drive to improve things alongside a genuine love of coming to work for all those you are leading is the aim. Having clarity and consistency is key and a shared moral purpose then ensuring that all areas of your organisation reflect the commitment to the work you are trying to do is the toddler equivalent of 'getting the shoe on the correct foot'.

2. *Mine!* Hold on to what is important to you

There is a phrase that in the history of phrases is up there with quite frankly the most ridiculous ever. The phrase is: 'It's like taking candy from a baby.' Well, if you've ever had the misfortune to be in the position of trying to remove a packet of chocolate buttons or a lollipop from the sticky vice-like grip of a toddler, you'll know that this phrase is not appropriate for describing something which is easy. Taking candy from a baby requires the same degree of skill as an internationally trained hostage negotiator or the role of peacekeeper at the UN. Toddlers will grip with grim determination and a phenomenal strength of character and this will ensure that any challenge to remove the chocolate – however skilled or strategic – is ultimately doomed to failure.

It is this 'holding on', that as leaders we also need to develop. To the toddler in that moment, it's often not about the chocolate, it's about something bigger, about independence and their own vision of what they want for their future – to smear chocolate all over their face, in their hair and to delight in it all. They are not bound by the social niceties and conventions such as knowing that an echoey post office full of disapproving tutters is not the place to exercise your vocal cords or to 'pushchair plank' – they are not to be swayed by simple pleas or even bribery. They are not cowed by a 'no', nor defeated by a 'maybe', an 'if', or other conditionals designed to get them to curtail their often-ear-splitting onslaught. They are clear about what they want, and they are determined to achieve results.

Now I'm not saying that in leadership we should lie prostrate and wail every time we encounter a challenge that doesn't align with our aims, but what we should do is have the courage to hold on to what's important to us, we must 'hold the line'. But how do we decide what is important to us? How do we pick our battles? How do we know when to sit docile in our pushchairs and watch the world go by and when it is timely to release the chocolate resilience and lollipop battle mentality? It's about knowing what's important to you and to your organisation.

31

It's easy to see every event in leadership, which doesn't align perfectly with your vision, and its rollout as a problem that needs fixing or challenging immediately and to begin firing on all cylinders. It's also as easy to agree to taking on every new idea and initiative in kind of 'fear of missing out' frenzy.

This will lead to one of two scenarios:

1. Picking up every misalignment in the beginning, however small, will take focus off the bigger picture and mean than nothing gets 'fixed' in its entirety. This 'whack a rat' style lack of focus and communication means efforts become centred on minutiae, and in that space the clarity of the bigger picture is lost.
2. The second is that the system becomes overloaded, muddled and lacking in clarity because the vision becomes too crowded with other pieces of work or ideas.

In the first instance, it's a little like setting a journey to drive from London to Edinburgh but constantly focusing on and becoming fixated by the state of the traffic jams in the Midlands or the quality of the service stations along the way and exerting effort to fix these. This is not the focus of the journey. The journey is to get to Edinburgh, although I wouldn't ever recommend this type of road trip with a toddler. No amount of lollipops and chocolate buttons would make that journey any kind of bearable! In the second instance, it is a little like supermarket shopping, which is again not ideal if you happen to have a toddler in tow. You may go in for bread and eggs and milk but come out with multiple BOGOF offers on nappies, coffee and baby shampoo but have totally forgotten the ultimate purpose of the shopping visit because you were distracted by other more interesting, brightly packaged or enticing ideas. So, as a leader we need to identify which strands of our work are our lollipops or chocolate buttons. Which are the elements of both our day-to-day focus *and* our long-term vision? Which are the important bits? If we can articulate in one – or at the most two – sentences what we are trying to achieve then this will ultimately make it more memorable, not just for us but also for everyone who works in our organisation. It also gives us a handy filter for deciding if something is worth doing when we consider a new idea or approach that is presented to us.

If we think of the decision filter like a giant funnel with a wide opening at the top and the narrow neck at the bottom, what we want to filter out is anything that doesn't ultimately help us achieve our core purpose and main body of work. There may be multiple excellent ideas being presented and poured into the top of the funnel, but it may not be an excellent idea for your organisation at that time in your current context and, therefore, needs filtering out. It's a little like hand-me-downs from a well-meaning friend for your toddler. They may be great, and they may well be used in the future, but they're currently the wrong size. Just because they're good quality items of clothing, doesn't mean you're going to put them on your toddler today and let them trip over gigantic trousers legs all afternoon and crack their head open on the coffee table. Great ideas are often still great ideas in the future. What can make a great idea go bad is when they're applied in the wrong context at the wrong point with the wrong focus at the wrong time. So, part of leadership is the clarity of thinking in terms of deciding what are your chocolate buttons and lollipops?

Identifying your chocolate buttons and lollipops:
- Can you summarise what you're trying to achieve in one sentence or three short bullet points? Can all staff articulate it, and do they understand it? How do you know? Do all other stakeholders understand what you're trying to achieve? Do people know *how* it should be achieved? Are they clear on core practices and processes and do they feel capable and confident enough to play their part?
- Can you pinpoint what evidence has led you to choose these areas as your areas for focus? Why does this actually need doing? Why did it become the core focus of your work? What will be different as a result of it being achieved and why is this important? Will it still be important in three years' time or is it actually a short-term issue rather than an enduring and strategic development?

- Are your chocolate buttons delicious enough? Have you been ambitious enough and created a real vision (remember the delight of the chocolate covered toddler) or are you communicating about service stations and traffic jams? Have you clearly delineated between the actual vision towards which you are all working and then the smaller actions needed to get there? Do people understand why it is important to do this work and are they equally motivated to achieve it?

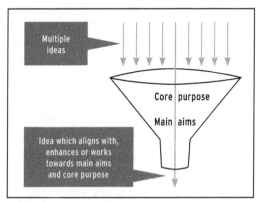

The decision filter

Once we've identified our chocolate buttons and our lollipops and think about every future decision as passing through our filter, then holding onto what is important becomes easier and much clearer, as does having the confidence to reject those ideas which don't fit our vision. And if ever you're in any doubt whether a job is actually worth doing, look at it as whether it's one which will get you towards one of your chocolate buttons or is it a sticky fluff-covered dubious peppermint dredged up from the bottom of the change bag, because that's much easier to say no to. Identifying what's important to you and your organisation and that it's communicated clearly is the first key part of implementing any change. Holding the line and maintaining clarity and direction towards the change are the next steps. A clear filter for decision-making along the way will maintain a focus on ensuring that the right things are done at the right time for the right reason.

3. *Celery is yucky!* Being resolute in your stance

My children have an aversion to celery. Its very existence in the universe appears to be an affront to all three of them. Although I spend a disproportionate amount of my life sorting the squabbles between them that result from the things on which they cannot agree, on the subject of celery they are united. Needless to say, from the moment I lay my hand on it in the supermarket to the point at which I serve it up (heavily disguised in multiple concealed sauces and casseroles) my children are more than a little vocal about their strongly-held opinions about this otherwise innocuous vegetable. The vehemence with which they voice their opinions about my attempts to introduce it to their daily diet is impressive and nothing I can say, do, fricassee, dice or blend will change their minds. In their view 'celery is yucky' and on this, as a united trinity of celery haters, they will not budge.

It is this resolute standpoint that we as leaders need to develop. However, unlike the utter inflexibility and congealing outcomes of the teatime celery standoff, in leadership there needs to be a little give and take but ultimately we do need to become effective at – if we are to consider ourselves effective leaders – being resolute in our stance when it comes to the big decisions and doing what is 'right'. Often in leadership there are times when what is right and what is easy are not the same thing. Sometimes doing the right thing is the hardest thing of all to do. Unlike refusing to even look at a celery stick, sometimes we do have to tackle things head on and simply do the right thing. This calls for confidence and courage in our convictions, which in the often lonely position of leadership can regularly be in short supply.

As leaders we put ourselves out there as able to problem solve, to lead, to set the path, chart the course and know what to do at all times, but no one person is capable of solving and anticipating all problems and challenges that may come our way so we need to call on the expertise of well-developed and equally resolute teams. In headship I have had problems as diverse as flooded buildings, asbestos discovered under the main school floor, children stuck in railings, parental fist fights in the playground, social care emergencies with children in grave and immediate danger, and on one occasion a gargantuan swarm of bees which settled on the gates to the playground just as the classes were dismissed for morning break. I could not have solved any of these problems alone and without caling on knowledgeable colleagues with expertise in specialist areas. As the vision was shared and well communicated (we all knew our lollipops and our chocolate buttons) the leadership was not derailed by crises where the senior teams had to solve every problem alone, but confident and motivated staff working together to solve the majority of issues.

As well as all these situations, which required immediate action, there are also the ongoing rumbling issues that take up time, headspace and emotional energy. The escalating parental complaint. The working with a colleague who is consistently underperforming. Dealing with a much-loved member of staff who is undergoing complex and difficult health issues. Fighting to access support for a child who requires additional and specialist provision but is tangled in a web of red tape. Revisiting squeezed budgets and rehashing staffing allocations yet again with reduced resources. All of these things have the potential to change the overall long-term direction of the work of the organisation and cause us to take our eye off the ball and its intended trajectory. It takes a regular and scheduled revisiting of and checking in with our aims and vision (our chocolate buttons and lollipops) to remind us of which battles we should be devoting the bulk of our energies and which are just bumps in the road we need to ride out. Revisiting our core purpose and vision also gives us the energy to become more resolute in our stance. This revisiting is like leadership refuelling. I often go to my parents' house for tea and my dad makes an excellent chicken soup (it contains celery so my kids are obviously not the greatest of fans) but whenever I eat soup with my mum and dad and sit at my childhood kitchen table of my childhood, it gives me a sense of quiet reconnection.

Revisiting the *raison d'etre* of your daily work through regular lived and purposeful reconnection with what you are trying to achieve is like soup for the leadership soul. It is so easy to become lost in the day-to-day busyness of leadership that we can lose sight of what we're really trying to do and achieve, and once we lose sight then it becomes harder to hold the line and maintain our stance – we begin to drift. If significant time and energy is going to be put into developing vision, goals, strategic plans and investment of staff time and cognitive and emotional energies into understanding and getting on board with the vision, then as leaders and teams we need to be ready to defend it and be resolute in doing so. When someone challenges our shared stance, we need to be ready to defend it with the same passion, consistency and unshakable belief with which my children view the existence of celery. If it was worth investing in as a vision for your organisation then it deserves the energy of consistency and defence when challenged so that everyone knows that should they present us with leadership celery they will be certain that we will take action! (Just don't chuck it all over the kitchen floor and hurl a spoon like a javelin in a celery-induced protest.)

So, let's think about our celery stance:
- What are the most important parts of our vision that we would wish to defend? Are there any contentious aspects (some of which may just be changes to things that have 'always been done this way') of what we are trying to do which we may need to have pre-prepared evidence of why we are doing something to share (case studies, research findings, data)? Does everyone understand the 'why' and the supporting evidence? Have we identified any groups or stakeholders who may need additional information, evidence or opportunities for discussion about why we are doing what we are doing in order to be on board?
- Are there opportunities for meaningful and real consultation during periods of change? Have any hard to reach groups had opportunities to be involved in the consultation? How have diverse voices from across the wider system, the organisation, the stakeholders, families, pupils

and communities been involved in identifying and shaping the vision? Is everyone clear on what the key elements of the vision are?

- Do teams in school have clearly defined roles and responsibilities? Is everyone clear on what part they play in not only day-to-day work but also in pinch points and crises? Are there clear processes for any complaints and clear systems and opportunities for airing opinions?
- Is there regular scheduled reconnection with core values and aims? Is this scheduled reconnection just for leaders or are there opportunities for staff and all stakeholders to constantly revisit and link their work to the vision and aims?

Once we've identified exactly why what we're doing is not necessarily the easy but definitely the 'right' thing to do, we can hold the line much more easily. Building teams who have diverse voices and a range of skills but who are united on the 'leadership celery' (just like my trio of celery haters) will ensure that, in pinch points and crises, the overall direction doesn't get derailed. Just as my three children are very different and diverse and rarely agree on a lot of things, on the thing that matters to them they are a united and resolute trinity. Celery is yucky. Oh well, I'll just have to try them with asparagus instead.

4. *But I'm a big girl!* Taking the risk

As a caring parent, you spend a lot of your life catastrophising about what might happen if you let you darling progeny climb that tree, jump off that wall or spend that first night sleeping away from you in their own room (although I obviously use the term 'sleeping' very loosely as my insomniac trio of sleep thieves are not very partial to any length of shut eye). You imagine everything from broken limbs to flashing blue ambulance lights, vigils by hospital beds and wondering if you are doing long and lasting emotional damage by letting your child sleep away from the reassurance of a cot by your own bedside. Every milestone and every decision is often fraught with overthinking, worst case scenarios and second-guessing (often made even worse by the ravaging effects of prolonged sleep deprivation caused by the sleep haters in the first place). However, our toddlers are unencumbered by this mental load and skip lightly and freely from challenge to challenge, readily embracing new skills and new thinking every day without the risk albatross weighing heavy around their necks and squawking noisily in their ear telling them it'll all end in tears or at the very least a trip to the walk in centre. Observe any toddler and they'll not be totting up points on a risk assessment or second guessing their selections of playmates before they dive into their next challenge. They centre themselves fully and wholeheartedly in the moment and just blinkin' well have a go. By contrast, as adults we are constrained by the fear of what others may think, are aware of our own shortcomings and have the fear of failure looming large on many of our horizons. These are aspects of our thinking which simply do not feature in much of our toddlers' approaches to new challenges and this is one reason why they learn at such a startling rate. They constantly challenge themselves and surprise us as their parents that they can in fact do something which we thought completely impossible. Imagine that we were equipped with the unselfconsciousness and bravery of a toddler in our everyday working lives. Imagine if instead of thinking, 'That can never be done because of X, Y, Z', we thought to ourselves, 'But I'm big! I can do this!'

In many aspects of leadership there will be elements of risk. From appointing new staff to deciding how to deploy funds or utilise buildings, there will always be an element of risk. Doing something different is often a risk in itself, especially if there are long engrained and entrenched ways of doing things. Change is nearly always initially uncomfortable, but it rarely ends up in the kind of outcomes our internal catastrophising would have us believe. If we align our actions with our visions and aims (our chocolate buttons and lollipops) and we can articulate why we are taking the risk or making the difficult change (the leadership celery) and we have built teams with aligned visions, varied skills and well-understood aims, then risk in itself becomes less of a risk. It becomes an adventure and that is what a lot of leadership should be about –

adventuring. Just as our toddlers spend the day discovering new and exciting things that we didn't believe them to be capable of, so too should our leadership do the same for our organisation. We should ultimately be leading our organisations and people to places they never believed they could reach. We need to encourage our risk albatrosses to fledge and to encourage less catastrophising. We should be leading to adventure not to the ennui of predictability and more of the same. To do this we need to take the risks to say, 'Look, at us, we can do this!'

Be more toddler. Take the risk.

Reflecting on risk:

- If you could look into a magic mirror and see your organisation looking back at you in its most perfect state, what would you see? Have you got a clear vision of exactly what it would look like, feel like, stand for, not tolerate, or be known for?
- Have you listed the reasons why you think the above vision cannot happen? Are these reasons due to external accountability measures or lack of resources or are they actually possible if you do something different?
- Have you talked with stakeholders and advisors about how your vision might actually be possible? Have you explored widening your professional networks to see if other organisations have done similar projects with similar risks from which you can learn?
- Are your staff and stakeholders on board with the vision, however risky? Who is likely to object? What are the main objections? What are these objections rooted in (tradition, fear, lack of resources or funding, lack of willingness to change, lack of understanding or background knowledge)?
- Have you done a projected risk assessment of your plans? Have you rated the potential impact of any changes or investment and what would be the impact if it did go wrong?
- What would be the benefits of taking the risk both in the immediate timeframe, the near future and long term?

5.101 Gruffalos: Cultivating an ongoing love of reading, learning and language

Once, with absolutely zero success, I tried to convince a cohort of more than 40 young, newly qualified teachers that I watched *Love Island*. It was an unmitigated disaster and they saw straight through my utterly fabricated claim. I admitted to the actual truth being that I had watched approximately five minutes of it and was completely bemused. In fact, I told them it reminded me very much of tea, bath and bedtime in my house with my three very small children, what with the fact all I could see on *Love Island* were lots of people wandering around in either their pants, fancy dress outfits, mostly crying, all in and out of the wrong beds and with quite a lot of tired and emotional outbursts. You see wrangling three very small humans through the end of day exhaustion of mealtimes, clean ups, pyjamas, teeth and then trying to get them all to stay in bed requires herculean effort and the stealth and strategy of an MI6 agent. However, there is one part of the day which makes the disaster zone of the landing and the bombsite that is the post-tea kitchen seem not just bearable but actually a highlight of the day. Because there is simply nothing like seeing the joy on a child's face when they become utterly engrossed and captivated by a bedtime story or you find them snuggled under their duvets with a contraband torch because they loathe to leave any page unread or any picture unexplored.

How is it then that as adults and as leaders we all too often neglect the joy of learning and the escapism of being fully lost in something that captures our imaginations and fires our creativity? Evenings frequently find us wedded to our laptops or our smartphones, tired eyes blinking in blue light to the percussion of weary fingers, adding 'just five more minutes' to the logjam of hours already punched that day. Personal development, intellectual growth and the adding to our knowledge and oracy canons are all too often relegated to the 'one day', 'the holidays' or the 'someday, maybe never'. If we are to be leaders of learning, then we need to practise what we preach and be voracious in our appetites for constant learning and improvement, and we cannot do this locked into a spreadsheet or agonising over the wording of yet another email. We cannot leave the development of ourselves and the kindling of our intellectual fires to languish damp and defeated like a hurriedly discarded towel on the landing floor. Our toddlers prioritise their own learning and any parent who has read *The Gruffalo* for the hundred and first time will not fail to have recognised the staunch concentration, the silent whirring of a thousand tiny wheels of cognition as our toddlers model exactly how development occurs whilst snuggled under duvets and clutching stuffed animals. And sometimes we need to follow their lead.

We need to immerse ourselves in the books, the articles, the learning which fires our intellectual curiosity and keep us fresh in our thinking and wanting to go that extra mile. We don't see our toddlers rounding off their day bemoaning themselves that they did not tick off everything on their to do lists, and thus opting to stay up long into the night to practise their spoon feeding or button fastening. They don't deny themselves the opportunity to learn and to grow just because they didn't complete everything. Investment and focus on improving yourself and your knowledge as a leader is grossly underrated and all too often overlooked, but if we are to ever move ourselves and our organisations forward, we need to learn and to grow and to find the kind of thinking which makes us want to reach for that contraband torch or to read just one more chapter. A motivated and interested leader makes for a motivated and supportive team and a positive environment in the workplace. Neglect your own development and intellectual wellbeing and it can be a one-way ticket to the workplace resembling the exhausted and emotional high drama of *Love Island* or in my case, the noisy, plastic duck filled chaos that is baby and toddler bedtime.

Questions to consider:
- How much professional learning or study do your staff in different roles take part in? Does this amount change as they move through your organisation?

- How much professional study do you take part in? What was the most thought-provoking piece of professional learning you have engaged with recently?
- What would you like to find out more about for your own interests?
- What would you like to find out more about in order to benefit your organisation?
- What was the last book you read which was not linked to your work?
- What was the last book you read which was linked to your work?
- How often do you read for pleasure?
- How often do you read for study/professional learning?
- Who is in your professional learning network?
- Are there diverse voices to challenge and encourage debate around your decision-making and thinking?
- How often do you discuss professional learning with your teams?
- How much of what you are studying, and learning is to develop your own interests and passions and how much is procedural seeking only to find the answer to a problem?

6. *Are we there yet?* Checking in, not checking up

I loathe long car journeys. Not only am I almost always travel sick, I now seemingly always have to travel with a bag the size of a small county stuffed full of snacks, wipes and soothing distractions at my cramped feet and my children appear to use car journeys to exorcise gastrointestinal demons to ensure that maximum disruption is caused to any planned route and supposed arrival time. I remember one particularly hideous journey to a well-known forest holiday village. I was only a few weeks postpartum with my youngest, our middle one was in the middle of potty training and our eldest was only five. Because our car at the time couldn't fit three large infant car seats across the back, I ended up wedged between the baby and the toddler with a cool box containing a breast pump, storage bags and ice packs by my feet and a potty shoehorned near the back of my head in the absolutely rammed boot whilst the five year old sat up front with her dad. We ended up stuck in traffic for hours on end, which meant I had to repeatedly and painfully express on the A46, all whilst entertaining a toddler and a newborn who were wedged in their car seats. My eldest, delighted to be in the front with daddy was busy counting lorries and observing the effects of the gale-force winds that had whipped up. We were sat there so long that our cleverly planned supermarket click and collect slot had expired and I was frantically trying to call the supermarket to hang onto our order as it contained all the nappies, food and toiletries we couldn't wedge into the already overstuffed car. This was all whilst still pumping and attempting to entertain the two youngest in the back. Things really took a turn for the worse in the next half hour though when our potty training toddler needed to use my headrest potty. This meant my husband was crouched in a lay-by hanging onto a toddler who was seated precariously on a lurid pink potty in a gale whilst I was attached to a breast pump and waved self-consciously to lorry drivers who were peering into the chaos of our car. This was only superseded by the journey home from the holiday where my eldest was spectacularly sick over the dashboard, in the footwell and all over my husband as we sat in stationary traffic on yet another motorway. As we got out to try and wash her down and sort her out, the baby did one of those urban myth poos, which erupted out of the sides of the car seat like some hideous yellow volcano and filled the back passenger footwell.

By this time we had run out of muslins, tissues and wipes and so were having to scoop everything out with our bare hands and the kids' hoodies. This meant my toddler was now the only one not covered in something vile, which she rectified when we finally reached the sanctuary of a Little Chef and commandeered their toilets. She chose this venue to drop her entire meal in her lap, bypassing the bib completely. Add to this that it was over 30 degrees and so returning to the boiling car was not a pleasant experience. We had also somehow managed to bury all of the kids' spare clothes at the bottom of the overstuffed boot and so ended up in an out of town shopping park on the outskirts of Coventry in a branch of Next where we had to buy new clothes for everyone as we still had hours to travel home and everyone smelt like either a sewer rat or fermented cheese.

My husband and I still shudder when we talk of that holiday journey. In fact, it has become a thing of legend in our house. Whenever we think a day out is going badly we reminisce about that journey and it adds a great deal of perspective. However, if you ask our kids about that journey, they have a slightly different take on things. They remember the excitement about being on the road with mummy and daddy. They remember how great it was to have mummy in the back or to sit up front with daddy. They remember the fun game of 'count the windsocks', which my husband invented in desperation during the gale on the outward leg. They talk about how they tried to see the sea (even though we weren't going to the seaside) and they definitely don't talk about how many times they asked us 'Are we there yet?'. Despite the chaos, derailings, the sick, the potty in a gale and the detours, they simply remember the stages of the journey and the focus on the 'getting there'.

Although most journeys aren't quite as spectacularly multi-coloured as that one, the enduring refrain of 'Are we there yet?' is a constant companion on most of our journeys. As my children have got a little older, this has developed into other variants such as: 'How many minutes?', 'Are we going to nanny and granddad's house?', 'Is this as far as nanny and granddad's house?', and 'How long is ten minutes?'. My children (like most children) are obsessed with tracking the duration of a journey; they check in every few minutes, sometimes almost relentlessly, to reassess where they are and how long it will take to get there. As they have got older, it has become much easier to explain exactly what our location is and our proximity to our final destination – it really is no fun trying to explain to a two year old, who has no concept of time or the duration of a minute, just how long it will take to get to their sister's cross-country event on the other side of the county. But it is this checking in and focus on a final destination that we, as leaders, need to learn from.

Despite having no concept of time, our toddlers are always focused on the final goal or destination and regularly want to check in to make sure they are on track and are still focused on the main goals. They are not derailed by chaos or deterred by potties, gales and exploding car seats; they remain positive, unbowed and will happily count windsocks as long as it gets them to where they need to go. As leaders we need to be mindful of our own checking in, that it doesn't become micromanaging of systems or processes and focusing too much on minutiae, which can be demoralising and promote a culture of mistrust and a lack of autonomy. However, we do need to check in regularly to see if we can see the sea yet. We need to structure opportunities for conversations that allow and encourage people to explain their thinking, their approaches and their impact within the frame of our vision and our 'chocolate buttons'.

When 'checking in' becomes 'checking up', then positive culture, autonomy and trust is eroded. In this sort of culture, you're going to get stuck in traffic as we lose sight of what's important and how we want to move towards that ultimate destination. When our deliberate checking in becomes conversations about what is working well and having impact and what might need to change in order to keep on track and to move more effectively and swiftly towards the sea, then this is where everyone understands how long ten minutes is and that they can seek support to help them along the way. Of course, there are measures that are hard data and which can be neatly put into a spreadsheet to check up on, you can count windsocks in a gale all day long though but it won't help you reach your destination any more quickly. When you build a culture of trust you also build resilience for when the journey takes a sudden turn for the worse. Staff who feel genuinely trusted and valued in an organisation will always be more confident to take risks, especially when this is twinned with clearly communicated destinations, values, expectations and processes. Sadly, too many leaders focus on the managerial aspects of 'checking up' and not the leadership aspects of 'checking in'. We want to create organisations where people don't need to consult weighty tomes outlining exact systems, procedures and policies and are fearful of bringing innovation or challenge to the table because it conflicts with the significant micromanaging rulebooks. We want to create a culture where everyone wants to see the sea and they want to check in to see that they're on track, not be scrutinised or called out for some insignificant misapplication or misjudgement.

What we want to develop is a well understood 'checking in' and clearly communicated expectations across our work. Do we all understand what we would expect to see in terms of behaviour at different points during the day? Do we all know what's expected in terms of curriculum coverage or pupil talk in class? Once expectations are clear, these should be a guiding set of principles and a lens through which we encourage staff to check in with themselves and to discuss ways in which we can improve the journey for everyone. It is interesting that our toddlers ask, 'Are *we* there yet?' as opposed to 'Am *I* there yet?' They recognise that within the car there are different people with different roles (I am always keeper of the snacks; my eldest now dictates the soundtrack) but they implicitly recognise that despite the different roles, we are all in it together and we are all ultimately heading in the same direction and will arrive at the same time, whether that be bright, breezy and with a boot full of click and collect shopping, or exhausted, covered in unmentionable fluids and with a boot full of Next bags stuffed with filthy, stinking clothes from a Coventry car park. However difficult the journey and however far we need to take our organisation, we must always focus on whether we can all see the sea and not on counting windsocks. Once we ensure that our work, our conversations and our efforts are on ensuring 'we' all get there, and we all know where we're going, then any journey becomes a lot more focused with fewer detours and hopefully no potties in a gale.

7. Raffle tickets, swimming kits and nappy bags: How to ensure everyone knows what's going on

Most of my life as a parent of three small children seems to be 80% packing, unpacking and repacking various types of bags: swimming kits, nursery bags, playgroup lunches, violins, reading packets and PE kits to name a few. The list is endless, as is the associated paperwork: permission slips in abundance, newsletters and requests for everything from harvest donations to tombola prizes. Indeed, my children arrive home from their various days and I just get paper thrown at me like confetti at a wedding.

Having quite a few near misses over the years in terms of almost forgetting World Book Day dress up activities and on other occasions trawling through the cupboards five minutes before we're due to leave in search of something half decent for the EYFS class hamper, in recent months I have capitulated and admitted defeat. I've bought a whiteboard for my kitchen. On it, in beautifully organised columns, is each child, their day of the week and their associated social, childcare and educational commitments. I stand in front of it most mornings, feeling either smug that I remembered to iron the shirts for photo day or cursing myself for not remembering where I put the shin pads but, either way, I'm clearly informed on what I need to do to get us all out of the door and to the right place at the right time with (hopefully) the right gear. Nonetheless, I have lost count of the number of times I've made the lunch for playgroup and had to leg it back home to get it as I've actually left it in the fridge. The mental load of three small children and a job breaks even the most loyal whiteboard devotee on occasions!

And there is a lot that goes on in terms of importance in those bags. Those bags can decide the success or otherwise of everything from the most mundane car trip where you forgot to pack the dummy, so the entire trip is an ear splitting furious shriek of frustration from the baby, or something slightly more embarrassing like the time we went to Thomas Land at Drayton Manor and I thought I had loaded up the pram with everything we could possibly need. I was prepared for everything from a scorching heatwave to a monsoon or a nuclear event. I had everything from five sets of full body waterproofs, sunshades, sunscreen, sunhats, picnic blankets, plasters, enough snacks to see us out for a fortnight, hairbrushes, dummies, changes of clothes. I had pretty much wedged the entire house underneath and off the handle of the pram. I wasn't so much pushing a buggy as a caravan with a week's worth of luggage. In fact, I'd had to pack so much that I'd had to find a much bigger bag, as well as additional lunchboxes and carrier bags. We got to Thomas Land, navigated the family toilets (which are incidentally absolutely amazing) and were just about to get on one of the rides when the youngest did his party trick of completely filling his nappy. It was then that I was struck dumb with horror. Despite having brought half of our house with us, I'd actually forgotten to bring any nappies at all. Cue mad panic and lots of crying (almost mine) as the elder two wanted to go on the rides and I was freaking out that the pushchair was slowly filling up. I nipped into the family toilets which dispensed nappies, but unfortunately these were only newborn size. By this time the baby was now yelling as well as the other two. I had to dash over to a family who had a baby who looked about the same age as ours and ask if I could buy some nappies off them as I'd been such a doofus. The mum was lovely and gave me a handful from her massive sensible stash and refused to take any money for them at all. I'll never forget how lovely she was and how she reassured me that we'd all been there.

After we had sorted the little one out and finally got the elder two on the rides it made me realise how our intention, our vision to have the loveliest day out was almost scuppered by a lack of attention to detail and how because I hadn't made a list for myself, or asked anyone else to help me mentally check off that we'd got everything, that we ended up almost having an epic 'code brown' in the middle of Thomas Land. It's this kind of planning that can make things either work or collapse in leadership. I'm the kind of person who swings between utter perfectionist control freak and a mentality of 'let's just wing it; it's a great idea so it's bound to just be alright!' It's a bit of a deadly combination in that

I'm either micromanaging things or just busy dreaming up great ideas where I haven't thought through the detail. One of the reasons the co-headship model worked so well for me was that the opportunity to 'double check' every project was built in. If one of us had an idea, the other could question its structure, validity, approach, commitment, cost and the general prospect of it actually happening. It was a great model for ensuring that no one gets carried away with an idea without actually thinking through the detail, and in leadership there is so much detail that needs thinking about. There is a school of thought that leadership isn't about the detail and that that's management but realistically, especially in smaller organisations, there is a lot of leadership that is about the detail and about ensuring everything gets done. One of the best ways to avoid a leadership 'code brown' is to ensure you have rigorous systems to plan any change or improvement and that you enlist someone else to help moderate and talk through this organisation.

If I had asked my husband to help me run through a mental checklist that morning (like one of us always does for the other before we go out anywhere as a family) then it was unlikely I'd have ended up pleading with strangers for nappies. The importance of planning change, moderation and collaboration cannot be overstated as the smallest detail on occasion can completely derail your bigger vision. Our toddlers also like to know exactly what's happening. From a very young age all three of mine have asked if it's, 'nursery day' or 'gym day' or 'Kimble's day'. They also ask every morning for a run down of the day ahead. My youngest loves to know that we're taking the girls to school, then it's playgroup and lunch club, then it's home for a sleep, then it's playtime with mummy, then we'll get the girls and then we'll come home and have tea. He knows exactly what's happening at each stage of the day and he delights in knowing what's coming next. As he's got a little older, he'll go and get his wellies for the muddy walk to school or his nursery shoes if he knows daddy is taking him to nursery in the car. He's even started to ask me if I've remembered his lunch (he knows my foibles only too well) and will proudly tell anyone he chats with about what his exact plans are for the day. He knows what we need, what he's doing and what's likely to happen at any stage. He also gets annoyed if we have to deviate from it, demanding an explanation, and telling me in no uncertain terms that 'You said we were going to the park not the supermarket!' Believe me, I've tried selling the supermarket as exciting but it's just not the park and it wasn't my fault it started tipping it down with rain. Our toddlers' fastidiousness with regards to routine and planning is something we could all learn from.

Despite their love of novelty and their ability to find imaginative and wonderful approaches to the way they look at life, their success a lot of the time boils down to planning and routine. The way we approach some of leadership tasks could learn from this devotion to consistency and method. Paperwork and action planning was something I loathed in headship, but it was also absolutely necessary in order to get things done and to communicate ideas effectively. It was all very well having a great idea or a really clear vision of the new horizon you wanted to travel to, but unless this was communicated clearly and with a well-understood route and anticipated pitfalls, then everyone you were trying to involve could have been envisaging a completely different vista to the one you were gazing at.

The best action plans are those that outline how your key resources are going to be deployed and by this I don't necessarily mean money. Our most valuable resources in organisations are time and people. Sadly when people see a 'resources' column on an action plan they can fail to recognise the cost of exactly how long it will take to implement an action and just who will be involved in terms of their time and commitment to the project. Thinking through a change you want to make, however nimble you perceive it to be, will always take longer to execute than you think. This is because if a change is going to be effective then everyone needs to be aware of the information, the requirements, the vision and the 'why', and this can take time. This time can be reduced if you have a clear set of shared goals and a shared vision, 'your chocolate buttons', but change always requires stages of assimilation, testing, recalibrating and then finally adoption, and so will always require longer than many of us in leadership think. This is often because by the time we have come to an idea, we have been ruminating on it for some time and so understand it fully. Those of whom we are sharing it with don't necessarily have the luxury of living inside our heads and so, to many, the idea may be new and therefore require longer to understand and adopt. Just like the new idea of taking my family to Thomas Land seemed a marvellous idea for which I was super prepared, I had failed to enlist anyone else in the planning and decision-making so had almost inadvertently ruined the vision of a lovely day out.

Subsequently, any action plan should include time for discussion, aspects of group decision-making, and significant opportunities for the voices of other stakeholders, as well as clear indication as to who will monitor and report on the success of any change. Just like our toddlers can articulate the structure of their days, any effective action plan also needs to be simple. I have seen many action planning documents over the years that are huge weighty tomes narrating vast quantities of procedural information, which (because of their length) remain unread, useless and subsequently not worth the great swathes of paper they're written on. A great action plan is one that enables everyone to be like our toddlers, able to articulate where they're going, what they'll need and how it fits in with the rest of the day. When we write our action plans, we're writing them as an aide memoir for everyone to reference, not as a narrative of every minute instruction involved in the process. Where additional detail is needed for a specific section, appendices or references work well to separate documents and plans, but a really good action plan means everyone knows whether they need their shin pads, their wellies or some raffle tickets.

If as a leader, you fall into the 'disorganised winging it' camp, it's always good to find yourself a colleague or mentor, who my former co-head colleague referred to as 'a sock ironer'. This is someone who has absolute attention to detail in everything they do and is fastidious, persistent and tireless in their pursuit of anything requiring nit picking or precision.

There comes a time in any leadership role where you have to do a bit of cognitive offloading too and get yourself the equivalent of my kitchen whiteboard. If you're already carrying the mental load of caring for small children then a significant chunk of your brain will already be cluttered with PTA notices, playgroup dress up day information and the relentless stream of birthday parties. With this in mind, ensuring that you develop systems for not forgetting stuff is so important. I'm a bit old school in that I still love a notebook, a paper list and, on occasions, an email to myself so it's there when I open it up in the office. Others are far more tech savvy (I have the technical capabilities of a gatepost, in fact tech and I are like oil and water) and enlist the help of apps, online reminders and utilise electronic calendars.

Whatever you choose, it's so important that somewhere you also keep the list of the chocolate buttons. In our old co-heads' office we had a giant whiteboard which contained our scribbled to do lists and sudden brainwaves, but all over the office were also our key values and photos of the children in our school. This meant that every discussion and decision was guided by our core values and our reason for doing the work in the first place. I may moan constantly about the number of slips I have to fill in or miniature bags I have to pack as a parent, but I know that in the grand scheme of things I'm doing all of this for a long-term vision of my own three children having the best time I can give them and growing up to be decent, kind and well-rounded adults. If I didn't keep an eye on that longer-term vision then it would be easy to drown in the tedium of the mundane, neverending work of parenting prep. Keeping our 'eyes on the prize' whenever we communicate plans to staff or begin a project ourselves keeps everyone from feeling that they're simply packing another bag and instead can seem themselves as part of the bigger plan or a lovely day out at Thomas Land.

Lesson two: Building teams

1. *Watch me mummy!* Developing positive teams

There is nothing designed for relaxation and leisure which elicits so much blind panic and skipped heartbeats as a playground or park when you have a small toddler in tow. Before I had my children, I envisaged happy sunny afternoons with a chequered picnic blanket under a tree, whilst I read something intellectually life affirming and improving and my children swung, climbed and see-sawed happily, occasionally only interrupting my train of thought to bring me interesting specimens of leaves or caterpillars, which we would discuss together and marvel at the wonders of nature.

What actually happens when you have multiple small children at a park at any one time is that you spend most of it locating park toilets that are usually a grotesque plumbing abomination and the rest of the time lunging like an internationally capped goalkeeper to prevent your offspring gleefully faceplanting off a giant slide or enormous spider web climbing frame. You also become inducted into the ennui of swing pushing. This rite of passage for all parents involves hours of finger numbing, feet freezing grinning as you push your child backwards and forwards for what seems like millennia as they squeal joyfully, and you rue the fact you forgot to bring a thermal mug.

You will return muddied, frozen (or sweating dependent on the season) wanting a bath in Dettol thanks to the frequent trips to the park toilets and bemoaning the fact you forgot to put on the oven for the jacket potatoes for lunch. Your offspring however will be pink cheeked, claiming you are the best mummy ever and attempting to pull off mucky boots and hurling them on the porch floor before launching themselves into a little bit of lounge destruction.

It is a far cry from the dream of the picnic blanket under the dappled shade of a blossom filled apple tree but, nevertheless, you will all have got out of the house, had a bit of fresh air, hopefully enough exercise to induce an afternoon nap and you all did actually laugh an awful lot despite the state of the toilets and the duration of the seemingly endless swinging session. This will be due in part to the fact that much of the visit will have been spent celebrating, and I don't just mean celebrating the fact that you noticed the pile of dog poo by the gates before you trundled the pushchair through it or that the swing didn't actually have clumps of other people's mud all over the seat from their wellies. Throughout the trip there will have been squeals of delight, celebrations of new skills mastered and invitations to share success through shouts of 'Look at me mummy!'. You see toddlers are excellent at motivating us to see all the good which is going on. There is an unwritten rule that when all is quiet then something suspiciously bad is probably going on as toddlers are usually experts at narrating every small success they achieve in their day-to-day dealings. They are the first to run to us to tell us how they have managed to put on their own shoe or get the toy car to go through the toy garage door themselves.

They are so keen to show us and anyone else who will listen that they can drink from a cup without a lid or can reach the door handle all by themselves. The effects of this are that they build positive teams around them almost constantly as it takes a real hard heart not to congratulate a beaming toddler who has just mastered climbing the stairs or putting on their own hat. This unconditional positivity is what helps to build teams.

All too often in leadership we do not take the time to celebrate what is going well or, if we do, it is done with too many 'next steps' attached to it. This creates a seemingly endless 'unfinished' approach to anything that we or our teams may achieve. We analyse data and don't take the time to congratulate ourselves on a job well done, or on a piece of research or professional learning that bore fruitful results. We are so busy on the treadmill of endless quests for improvement that we don't take that moment at the top of the slide or the climbing frame to shout, 'Look how high I am!' We take it for granted that our teams will follow our vision if we implement it clearly and articulate it well, but we need to live and celebrate the living of our vision, not just watch from our chequered leadership blankets and cheerily give a wave now and then. We need to, like at the park, be in the thick of it, building teams by celebrating their ascents to the top of their slides, being there to notice if one of them is going to face plant off something and having an awareness of when to celebrate, when to motivate and encourage them to take the next steps, and when to simply gather everyone back together for a rest and a jacket potato.

We also need to be committed to all parts of the leadership role, not just the exciting ascents and the fun slides and roundabouts, but also the boring business of the swinging. There will be much of leadership and team building which is just the routine consistency of the backwards and forwards, but these interactions are often what keeps an organisation ticking over. The routine actions and dull aspects of the job still need to be done and they may take up what feels like hours but are nevertheless a key part of the role. Everyone's leadership 'swing' will be different too.

For some the job of finance and budgeting may seem unutterably dull, for others it is the tangled web and minefield that is HR, for others it will be board or governing body meetings, but everyone is sure to have one aspect of their role which is akin to the endless swinging. However, if the organisation is to function effectively and the other exciting parts of the leadership park are to be visited then this swinging still needs to be done. It is a real skill not to let your frustration with these tasks affect the positivity of the overall team too. Just like you would never moan endlessly at a toddler who was loving their extended time on the swing, you would never in leadership fail to give your full and most positive regard for those colleagues involved in the aspects of the job in which you find it most difficult to engage.

Just as we set the weather in our home lives with our toddlers, if we are snappy, tired or short with them then they will be nervy, confused and tearful, we need to remember that we set the weather in our leadership roles too. Our teams will take their lead from and be influenced by our attitudes to people, to success and to areas for development. To build positive teams we need to develop unconditional positive regard, which we need to extend to every aspect of our leadership parks and the people in it, from the excitement of the slides to the mundane swings. Every aspect of our leadership parks needs to be viewed positively, its successes celebrated and all should receive the same positive versions of ourselves and a willingness to get involved. However, I draw the line about being positive about those toilets!

Questions to consider:
- How are successes communicated and celebrated across our organisation?
- Are the successes of colleagues at all levels celebrated and communicated or just those in key positions?
- Are there scheduled opportunities to look at what is going really well and to discuss this as whole teams?
- How often is my leadership geared towards watching from a distance and how much of it is getting involved and seeing/feeling/hearing what an initiative or current work is like? (How often am I watching from a blanket or getting up to play on the park?)
- Which aspects of my job do I find most interesting and exciting? Which aspects do I find less interesting? Do the colleagues involved in my least favourite aspects see me demonstrate as much positivity as those in my favourite aspects of the job? How might I address this?

- How positive do my staff perceive me to be? How do I know this? Could I do some 360 feedback or other anonymous staff surveying? Am I aware of the impact of my own motivation on others?

2. *'Red sky at night, angel delight'*: How errors and how you react to them can be your most endearing quality when building teams

One of the funniest aspects of parenthood is when your child is mastering language. From the heart melting first 'mummy' to the pride of the first correctly used '*fank yoo*', there are endless lovely moments. However, when your toddler starts to speak more and begins to use language to communicate more about the world around them then that's where the real comedy moments come in. I remember coming home one evening from my parents' house with my daughter in the car. The sky was beautifully red and golden, and my daughter suddenly started jabbing at the window from her car seat and shouting, 'Mummy, mummy! Look!' I asked her what she'd seen, and she gave me a knowing look and said, 'The sky is red mummy and you know that means… red sky at night, angel delight!'

It still makes me smile every time I think about it. She was so certain she was right and so confident in her use of her version of the, 'red sky at night, shepherds' delight' that her version of it has since become the one we actually use as a family now. We could have simply told her she was wrong, corrected her and moved on but it was so comical that it became more than a learning point; it's also a point of reference and an ongoing part of our daily language alongside the correct version of it, of course. We were able to laugh about it, as she obviously didn't feel threatened or belittled by the pointing out of her mistake and that is something we often overlook when building teams.

We all too often forget in leadership that if we are to critique or correct someone's error, it is highly unlikely that that error is a deliberate one. In my background in education, I am yet to meet a teacher after 22 years of me being in the profession who deliberately wants to do a bad job. In fact, many teachers put in a staggering amount of energy, thought and time into the work they do, and we need to be mindful of this as leaders when we seek to discuss the effectiveness or accuracy of their work. Building a culture where mistakes are allowed and positive discussions stemming from them are championed are the ones where growth will occur. If we develop a culture where mistakes are to be shied away from for fear of being chastised or overly corrected, then there will be no creativity or movement. Just as toddlers don't master language overnight – there are subtle and small changes in their abilities to form individual sounds correctly, then words, then short sentences and then longer conversations – so too will the development of our organisations mirror this. If we want to bring about incremental change or development, we must refine the way in which we respond to mistakes or errors. If we are to effect a whole organisation change in the way that a toddler becomes fluent in formulating extended sentences, we must celebrate what has gone well and not fixate on what is wrong. This is not to say errors go unchallenged or uncorrected, but that instead we create a culture where we recognise that within a period of change and development there will be points of misinterpretation, misalignment, misapplication or just plain errors and that we recognise these will need to be unpicked, but that it needs to be done in the context of an overall supportive and positive culture with a shared understanding of what we as our teams and organisations are trying to achieve.

The way in which we model this behaviour ourselves as leaders will be instrumental in implementing this effectively. If we present ourselves as infallible then we are setting up an unobtainable standard for our colleagues to emulate or aspire to be, consequently setting the organisation up for a culture where fallibility is seen as a weakness. The ability to recognise your own strengths and weaknesses as a leader and to articulate this at the same time as modelling how you are always seeking to improve these is a key way in which to communicate the learning behaviours you want to develop in your teams. Mistakes happen when something new is underway or new challenges are taken on. It is rare for mistakes to occur in the mundane, the procedural or the regular. Mistakes tend to happen during first times, new challenges, changes, testing out of new ideas or when people are stepping up to do a role that they have not done before. And these are the exciting points for an organisation and the people in it. There is a saying that creativity lies on the border of chaos and as a leader we are often leading our organisations into what could be construed as or has the potential to be chaos, whether that be a staffing restructure or a new approach across an organisation. Whenever there is the possibility for creativity or risk is when we need to demonstrate our very best leadership and human behaviours. This is when we need to show we are fallible, be able to apologise and have the courage to nimbly and humbly change course when we realise something genuinely isn't working. If people follow leaders they trust then we need to be honest about our own capabilities.

We need to be ready to apologise, to listen, to discuss, to change tack when the course is not the right one, to say that we found something difficult or that we haven't yet come up with a solution. What people need from their leaders is someone they can trust and so trotting out leadership platitudes which allude to, 'everything is alright, nothing to see here, move along now', when it is clear to everyone that the wheels are coming off does not breed a culture of trust. The leader will continue to set the weather during periods of change as well as during calmer periods and the leader needs to set the precedent for behaviours during this, those of honesty, clarity, being realistic, being humble, being willing to get involved and having a go, maintaining positivity and having the courage to say when something isn't working.

Leadership is not about being perfection personified. It is about being optimistic and ambitious but also honest, realistic and humble. If you want to take people with you, be fallible, if you want to lead alone striding out at the front and followed tentatively by fearful teams, be perfect. *Red sky at night, angel delight.*

Questions to consider:
- Am I clear about what are my own strengths and areas for development?
- How have I come to develop this list? Is it from trusted feedback and analysis or just a hunch?
- How do I react when I discover something that is misaligned with an original plan?
- How will I encourage honest and open feedback from staff during projects?
- How do I communicate how I am currently developing and what my own strengths and areas for development are?
- How often are there opportunities to discuss what is going well, revisit the aims and to evaluate as a team how well everything is going?
- Is there a culture of positivity? How do I know? Do staff at all levels display confidence in risk taking, idea creation and are they clear about the importance and value of their contribution?

3. The potato forest and a cardboard box: Work with what you've got

In most homes housing a toddler there will likely be piles of lurid plastic, some flashing or noisy and defying even the most capacious of storage solutions, and thus spilling like a multi-coloured tidal wave over most lounge carpets or bedroom floors. Hours as a parent will be spent *ooo*-ing and *aah*-ing with your toddler about the magicalness of Iggle Piggle's boat or Peppa Pig's house and then you will spend a disproportionate amount of your evenings either tossing them back into the overflowing storage boxes or whispering expletives as you accidentally step on half a squeaky plastic egg. But often these toys are not enough to distract and entertain your toddler despite all of their flashing lights, pop out doors and endless jingles.

Despite your most enthusiastic efforts, sometimes your child is simply not interested in pushing a triangular prism through the hole in the shell of a pull-along turtle for the forty-sixth time that day. These are the days when imagination and creativity come to the fore not only for you but also for your toddler. Whilst attending to a slight vomit emergency with my middle child when she was a baby, my eldest was left in the kitchen playing happily for a while. When I came back down, she had foregone the pile of toys from the toybox and had created an elaborate game with a discarded cardboard box and a bag of new potatoes I'd left on the side. She proceeded to play with the bag of potatoes and the box for almost the whole morning, utterly engrossed in what she was doing and requiring no intervention, no additional toys and no extra help from me, which was handy as the baby had decided on that particular day she was going to try and smash the existing world record for most outfit changes in one morning due to what turned out to be a rather nasty bug.

It was watching her that I realised that sometimes you just have to work with what you've got. Unfortunately for her that day, because of her poorly baby sister, she had very little interaction with me as I spent most of it up to my elbows in soggy clothes, bowls of soapy water and antibacterial spray. She also had no want or use for her previous resources, her toys, as they weren't meeting her needs that day. She did however, have a couple of new resources with which to play and, although not traditional toys (I know all kids love a cardboard box but I'm not so sure on a bag of Jersey Royals), she entertained herself productively for hours.

I was mightily impressed with her resourcefulness and her ability to make the best of what was a pretty rubbish situation. It made me think that in leadership we often need to do exactly that, to make a potato forest out of a bag of spuds and a cardboard box. When we take on a new leadership role it is unlikely we can create the abundance of beautiful resources which match our needs perfectly, like the overflowing box of appropriate toys, it is far more likely that we will inherit something more akin to the potatoes and the box. However successful an organisation, the departure of one leader and the introduction of another will mean significant change for all involved and everyone will need to change and adapt what they're doing in order to accommodate this change in the leadership wind. What you do with the resources you have and how creatively you use these will help to determine the success of any leadership work you undertake. Your resources will be varied too, much more than just potatoes and a box. There are the physical resources and state of repair of any buildings or land. There is the decorative order and physical state of the internal rooms and shared areas. The practical and technological resources available for teams to discharge their duties will also need assessing, as will the harder to measure audits of the skills, experience and expertise of staff at all levels across the organisation. There is also the assessing of the almost invisible aspects of time and attitudes.

You may have all the physical resources in the world and a highly skilled staff team but if there is not that positive regard and will to make a difference, or if the current workload is so swamping that people simply don't have the time to make further changes or adaptations, then nothing will even get off the ground. Leaders need to be aware of exactly what they have at their disposal in order to drive through any change or improvement and to recognise that some of this is directly and easily measurable, such as the state of repair of a building or the age and efficacy of a computer system, but that other resources which have the potential to drive through and sustain change are not so measurable. Accurately assessing exactly what time, tools, attitudes, physical resources, financial resources, skills and knowledge you have will be the key to working effectively with what you've got. It'll be this ability and insight which, when aligned with your vision and plans, will help to turn a bag of spuds and box into a magical potato forest.

Questions to consider:
- What physical site resources do I have and what are the conditions of these? Buildings, land, parking, play equipment, access routes, fencing, etc.
- What internal resources do I have and what are the state of repair and decorative order of these? Classrooms, corridors, storage areas, meeting

spaces, toilets and washing facilities, cloakrooms, cooking and food prep/storage areas, offices, communal spaces, specialist facilities e.g. pools, therapy rooms, boiler rooms. Are they fit for purpose?

- What equipment do I have in order for everyone to discharge their duties? What is the state of repair of these and do they need updating or upgrading? Are they fit for purpose? Computer systems, mobile IT equipment, projection and presentation equipment, chairs, tables, seating, storage furniture, specialist equipment, such as musical instruments, reading resources, toys and play equipment. Are these fit for purpose?

- What human resources do I have? Have I done an audit of skills, knowledge and areas of interest or expertise? Are there pockets of untapped skill or knowledge in unexpected roles or departments? Are there people looking for additional challenges or to reduce their hours?

- How much time do I have in which to effect any change? How much whole staff training time do I have, or is it all booked up? How strategic and effective is current use of meeting or professional learning time? Have I audited the impact of professional learning, mentoring, coaching or other learning opportunities to see which has had most impact and which have taken the most time?

- Have I looked at timetabling and scheduling including deployment of staff to look at whether additional time can be created or redirected? Have I questioned why the current deployment model is in place? Is it because it has always been done like this or is it because it is the most effective way of doing things?

- Who do I have in my wider resource bank to help me? What networks, affiliations or professional relationships can I develop to help me?

- What do I currently have and what do I actually need in order to effect the intended change?

4. *I love you mummy*: Being confidently honest about your feelings at work and surrounding yourself with the people you love at home

Toddlers not so much wear their hearts on their sleeves as have a constantly scrolling and unedited version of their feelings projected on their faces at all times. There is never any doubt as to what a toddler is feeling at any one time. From the crumpled furrow of a disgruntled brow to the red faced, head thrown back wailing of the aggrieved to the sunburst of joy which radiates when they are happy, there is never any doubting what a toddler thinks or feels and there is a lot we can learn from this. Now I am not suggesting that we greet the prospect of a three-hour finance meeting in an overly hot office by donkey sobbing and pounding the table with our fists, or by refusing point blank to put our coats on as we simply do not want to go out to the car and drive to that compliance update briefing, but we do owe our staff and our organisations a degree of honesty and clarity about how we are feeling. We discussed in previous chapters how fallibility is a strength of leadership, well in the same vein, so is humanity. A leader who remains tight-lipped in the face of sudden tragedy or who takes no time to celebrate a positive outcome for the organisation and simply trudges on unrelenting to the next hurdle is unlikely to acquire a loyal and dedicated team around them.

I remember when a school I worked in had been in an Ofsted category for a number of years. I had joined the school mid-way through a number of years where they lived under the shadow of this label and were working tirelessly to come out of it through sheer dogged determination, a will to succeed and an unswerving focus on making things better for the pupils and community the school served. The day we came out of special measures was akin to a carnival crossed with the declaration of the end of a war. We were deliriously happy, relieved and delighted to have finally rid the shackles of special measures and wanted to celebrate the success and what had been the final point on an excessively difficult and emotional journey.

We were asked to assemble in the staff room where a senior leader from the local authority who represented our local authority maintained school at council level (but who didn't work with us) had called us for a meeting. We stumbled in, giddy with relief and high on the success we had just procured as a team. This leader – this person who had constantly told us we were not good enough but had not done anything practical on a day-to-day basis to help us – stood there in that staff room and said this: 'I know you're all really pleased that you've come out of special measures but there's still a lot of work to do. Here's to the next stage!'

Never in the history of my career to date has there been a more ill-timed or ill-judged piece of feedback from a leader. From collective smiles and joy there was an instant whole-scale shift to resentment and anger. This leader couldn't even take the time to congratulate the teams properly or to let us have our moment in the sun. I remember being so angry I could barely look them in the eye. They continued to talk for about 15 minutes, but I can guarantee that not one person in that room was listening to a single word they were uttering. In that moment they had destroyed the already fragile working relationship they had with an entire roomful of professionals and it was due to a lack of humility. This leader knew how hard we had worked. They knew the additional hours, passion and care with which so many of the team had given selflessly. They knew we'd missed family occasions, nights out with friends, our leisure time and our own sleep at night to ensure that we came through this, and yet this leader had decided that none of that was worth mentioning and all that mattered was 'onwards and upwards'. That one meeting taught me more than any other leadership training I've ever had.

By contrast, the unbridled joy with which the then deputy head greeted the news was a huge and startling contrast. He whooped his way around each classroom, gathering people up in hugs and lifting them off the ground, dancing on chairs, running with his hands raised while completing celebratory laps around the playground. His whole demeanour was pure joy and it was infectious. He congratulated each and every single person on every team at every level across the school. He beamed, he giggled, he high-fived and air punched his way from classroom to classroom, giving permission for everyone else to share in the outpouring of joy, relief and pride we all felt. It was he who then harnessed this to continue to move the school forward throughout the next few years.

The openness with which he had shared his passion for the school and the time he had taken to express his gratitude towards everyone who had contributed was a master class in openness and team building. Another colleague I've worked with whose qualities of humanity, humour, integrity and kindness were awe-inspiring was my former co-head colleague. Her ability to form warm, meaningful and honest relationships with staff in all roles and all levels stemmed from her own lived values of kindness and righteous indignation. She was never afraid to champion the underdog or to call out behaviour that made her angry or upset or made others feel that way. She would celebrate, commiserate, support and champion all staff and in return they knew they had a leader in front of them who was passionate about developing everybody. She has cried with staff through shocking personal tragedies in their home lives, been a champion and a voice for those who needed strength and has always been honest and full of humour about her own abilities and approaches. She too is a master class in leadership as she demonstrates through every action how leaders are humans first, leaders second. Because of this, her dedicated staff would follow her to the ends of the earth.

With leadership often being an emotional rollercoaster, it is important that our own reserves are restored and replenished in readiness for our work. It is all too often too easy to prioritise work over family or leisure time, but it is integral to our ongoing success as a leader that we can hang up our leadership cloak when we return home and become surrounded by the people and things which make us feel grounded, loved and calm and where we are loved unconditionally just for being us – our flawed and genuine selves – not simply admired or looked up to because we have a particular job. Sometimes we need to be all about the soul and not the role. Whether we find family time, leisure pursuits, reading or hobbies restorative, it is important for us to maintain genuine relationships with the people we love so that we can carry that with us when leadership waters are choppy.

There is much anecdotal and published evidence about the negative effects of working over a 50-plus hour week and there is just as much evidence about the health benefits of physical contact with those we love. Hugging our children and our loved ones releases serotonin and chemicals which are calming and have a positive effect on our mental and physical wellbeing, and you simply can't hug your kids properly from behind a laptop or from inside a lengthy meeting. Surrounding yourself with friends and family who know you as something other than the leader or the boss is also restorative. Family dynamics may mean that you are actually the baby of the family or you may have a friend or partner who likes to take charge of ideas and activities, which means that for at least some of your week you are not having to always be the leader or the boss, which can be utterly exhausting. Surrounding yourself with the ones you love and genuinely being in the moment with them will always have a positive effect on your wellbeing and ultimately on your effectiveness as a leader. We see this in our toddlers when they become tired, frustrated or upset, they seek the comfort of a trusted adult to reconnect, reflect and recharge before toddling off to their next adventure. We need to take our emotional refuelling guides from them and remember that everyone needs a hug, a quiet five minutes and a chance to tell those closest to you that you love them. We may love our work and it may be our passion but no one ever reflects on or looks back over their lives and says, 'Do you know what? I wish I'd done more hours at the office.'

Questions to consider:
- How would your colleagues describe your overall general mood? Does this reflect how you really feel?
- How much of your working week or weekend is spent doing or thinking about work? How much is spent with the people you most

want to be with? Are you happy with this balance? What steps could you take to enable you to redress any imbalance?

- Do you encourage people at work to be open and honest about their feelings? Are there adequate support networks in your organisation that people can access if they are feeling overwhelmed either by work or home? How are these signposted and communicated? Is there a staff member responsible for wellbeing? What training have they received and how effective is their work? How do you know?
- Do staff members openly share successes? Is there a culture of success sharing in meetings, communications with stakeholders and across the organisation?
- Do 'next steps' always accompany messages about success?
- How approachable are you? How do you know?
- How many of your most recent interactions with colleagues were to praise?
- Do you model a good balance between home and work life to your staff?
- Do you pursue hobbies and interests outside of working hours?
- Who do people approach if they are struggling or need support in your organisation?

Lesson three:
Developing yourself as a leader

1. *I'm a superhero!* Being proud of your achievements

The dressing up box in our house is a firm favourite with all three of my children. When I call them for dinner, I never quite know what the cast around the table will be, all I know is that it's rarely without a cape or two, at least one princess ball gown and a variety of hats. The commitment each of my children devotes to the roles their costumes hint at never ceases to amaze me too. They are perfect little method actors insisting that they cannot simply walk to and sit at the table but often simulating a flight in, with added sound effects or appearing suddenly and brandishing a sword from underneath a chair. The cast around our dining table often looks like a break in filming for a Hollywood blockbuster or sci-fi adventure, rather than a dinner and a catch up over a plate of Bolognese.

One of their favourite ever games to play as a three is 'superheroes'. The superpowers of each varies every day, depending on what they can rustle up out of the dressing up box and whose turn it is to have the sparkly cape, but they are never short of days to save or victims to rescue and they are incredibly vocal about their own superpowers. I've lost count of the number of times I've had to pretend to die whilst washing up or pretend to be frozen whilst wiping the table. Their confidence and utter belief that they can indeed be a real-life superhero is the bit that taught me about leadership. When they launch themselves off the sofa, they delight in beating their personal bests as to how far they can jump and how much they have improved. They race around proclaiming that they are super-fast and super strong, and I am frequently called away to witness further superhero dance moves or displays of wonky forward rolls and wobbly cartwheels. But how often do we as leaders celebrate what we are doing well beyond a nervous, mumbled, data-driven performance management meeting? How often do we share with people what we have learnt from our experiences or offer support to others? Somehow, we are shackled by a combination of imposter syndrome and modesty. No one wants to be seen as a show off, or worse still, be seen to get anything wrong after putting themselves out there, but we really do need to embrace our superhero if we are to improve even further and encourage those around us to develop themselves at the same time. Being proud of your achievements does not need to be about putting yourself or your organisation on a pedestal or proclaiming you are a beacon of excellence in a particular area, it can be as simple as aligning yourself with groups who do similar work and offering to share your journey. It always surprises me how many leaders underestimate the fabulous work their organisations are doing.

Unfortunately, frequently the opposite is also true that those who are overconfident and want to collect followers and praise like football cards are often the least effective at self-evaluation or true collegiality. As leaders we are often quick to praise the work of others and to identify what is great about other organisations, but we often do not afford ourselves the same positive regard. Every leader has a story to tell and often these stories can help and motivate other leaders both current and aspirant. Every working day in leadership will add to the canon of your leadership knowledge and skills, even sharing mistakes from which you learnt will be valuable insight for others. Once in leadership we need to remember that running and leading an organisation requires a vast array of skills, competencies and knowledge so once in a while, we need to come to the dinner table wearing our virtual capes and give ourselves a pat on the back over a plate of that Bolognese.

Questions to consider:
- What have been your biggest achievements in the last year at home and at work?
- What aspects of those achievements at work might be of use to someone else? Could you share your findings as a case study or join a network online to offer examples?
- Have you considered sharing your work or achievements at an event with other professionals through being part of a panel, presenting team, writing an article?
- If you list the things you can do/know/are confident in this year and compared this to how you felt last year, can you identify areas of personal growth and development?
- Does your appraisal or performance review model encourage a deep reflection on achievement, as well as identifying next steps?

2. How far can you throw a boiled egg? Every day is a learning day

Having a toddler is often like holding a jack in the box which, when it opens, has the capacity to ruin or make your day. They often do things that fill your heart with joy and pride. On other days they just fill your house with lots of mess and anti-social smells. However, every day with a toddler is certainly new and always entertaining. You never quite know how the day will pan out, regardless of how organised and well planned you have been. Let's take something as straightforward as a boiled egg. I remember the first time I placed a boiled egg in front of my eldest daughter when she was just over a year old and turned my back to reach for a spoon. I had to duck suddenly as the egg flew past my ear and smashed onto the back wall of the kitchen. My daughter had obviously thought this lovely rounded object was a little like a ball and seeing as we had spent the morning practising throwing, thought that this too was part of the game. Initially, I was a bit annoyed that I now had to scrape egg off the kitchen I'd only just cleaned but then I started laughing about what a ruddy good throw it had actually been. That kid had an amazing overarm lob and had got that egg to clear the entire length of the kitchen. Another time with my middle daughter, I gave her her first boiled egg during a lunchtime when her older sister was at playgroup. This time, I demonstrated how to dip the spoon in and helped her with her first few mouthfuls. I turned my back to make myself a cup of tea and asked, 'Do you like your egg?' Her response was, 'I don't like the crunchy bits!' Puzzled, I turned around to find she'd eaten the rest of the egg in record time and had pulled the shell out of the egg cup and was trying to eat that too. Once again, despite my best planning, things didn't go as I expected. And this is another lesson for leadership. Every day is a learning day in a leadership role. You can plan and anticipate all you like, but you can guarantee that there will always be a curve ball of some unexpected form which will mean that things become stalled or temporarily derailed.

These learning moments come in many forms from personal realisations about your own strengths and limitations to life lessons, about how people react in different situations, or they may simply be a more practical lesson about the correct procedure for something you're doing for the first time. One guarantee though is that you will learn something new every day. There will not be a single day in leadership where you come away thinking the day has been mundane, repetitive or predictable. You never quite know whether the egg you present that day with will come whistling back at you past your ear or will be used in another totally unique and shell-crunching way. Your attitude to this constant leadership learning will be another factor in your success. You can either focus on the fact that you have an egg to scrape off the back of the kitchen wall or you can recognise that the egg chucking has actually revealed a real talent.

My eldest daughter has turned out to be an excellent athlete in track and field events, and that egg throwing was our first indication that this kid could chuck things one hell of a long way! When we encounter something new or different with our staff we can use the information we glean in much the same way. The way our teams react in an unexpected crisis or pressured situation, or the way they respond to additional responsibilities or new learning experiences, can show us so much about their own strengths and talents, and can lead to us deploying and developing them much more effectively in the future. In the same way, when different experiences reveal gaps in their knowledge and skills, we could see this as a problem, or we could see this as an opportunity to put in supportive development opportunities. We must also recognise the stamina required to lead and to be constantly learning in a leadership role. When there is a lack of predictability and lots of decision-making and learning to do every day it takes a toll on our mental, emotional and physical reserves. Just as toddlers are often exhausted after a day of learning at nursery or playgroup, so too are we. As leaders we need to recognise that learning takes up great cognitive and physical resources and we need to plan our diaries and work schedules to try and ensure that there are periods of calm and an ebb and flow to each day, week and term if we are to maintain the stamina to be ready for this leadership learning each day.

One of the hardest lessons I learnt early in leadership was that saying 'no' is necessary to preserve my effectiveness. It is imperative that gaps are left in the diary to catch up both with admin and thinking time. It occurred to me when I took my children swimming that the lifeguards at the pool took regular and scheduled breaks to recover from the heat and noise of poolside and to ensure they had a break from the important and intense vigilance and awareness required by their role. But how often do we act like lifeguards in our leadership roles? How often do we let ourselves step away from poolside to think, to catch up and to ensure that when we return, we are ready, up to date and not mentally occupied with that sinking feeling of a to do list weighing heavy on our minds? Part of leadership learning is that we need to ring fence our own time for planning, thinking and catching up. Moving out of the classroom meant that initially I felt I would have so much time in which to complete the leadership work. The fact of the matter is that, just like in parenting where you are responsible 24/7 for the children, so too do colleagues expect you to be available. If you are not strict with yourself in managing your own time and availability, scheduling in ring fenced admin time, or dedicated professional study and development time, you will end up like an exhausted lifeguard – hot, bothered, ineffective and unable to maintain the overview of the safety and function of the pool and its users.

In short, you'll be like those eggs were, in pretty hot water.

Questions to consider:
- What are your key priorities for learning in your leadership role? Are these procedural-based tasks, how to build effective working relationships, knowledge about the organisation's history and previous successes, new approaches to current work, research and best practice, networking? Have you articulated or listed not just what you have to do but what you want to learn? How often do you review this?
- Have you analysed your diary and commitments to ring fence time for finding out, reflecting, reading and analysing? How much of your diary time is blocked out for you to develop your own professional learning and to carry out the tasks necessary for you to undertake your role effectively?
- How well do you know the skills, talents and knowledge of your teams? Have you got a potential undiscovered champion egg chucker on the staff?

3. *I want to do it, 'on myself'*! Resilience, determination and the will to succeed

For reasons I cannot fathom, all three of my children have, at the same developmental stage, chosen to use the phrase, 'I want to do it *on* myself' rather than, 'I want to do it *by* myself'. It's always made me smile and even now I have to check my own usage of the phrase, so engrained in our family lexicon has the amended version become. But when I think about it in a leadership and development context, it too makes me smile because, as toddlers, the drive to become autonomous and capable and independent is evident in almost all that they do. Toddlers are rarely lazy when on the cusp of learning a new skill or system. They will happily let you put their shoes on for them for months, and then suddenly, when they realise that they might actually be able to do it alone, will (mood dependent) refuse to let you help them. They struggle, they get them on the wrong feet, they try to put them on backwards, they fumble with the fastenings, but they categorically will not let you help them. It is an interesting point to note too that this surge of independence and determination usually coincides with the exact point you are all desperately late and trying to get out of the door. You stand there sweating in your own coat, looking at your watch, panicking as to where exactly the car keys might be and calculating just how long you have left to let this go on before you risk a tantrum and wade in to complete the shoe putting on yourself. And this scenario has two lessons for us as leaders.

The first is that we should not be afraid to try new things for fear of failure. If we are 80% sure we can succeed at something, we should – like our toddlers – have a ruddy good go at it and keep on trying until we can get that shoe on properly. They will remain totally focused on the job in hand and will exclude all other extraneous noise or distraction until they have achieved their goals. How often in leadership do we deem things unobtainable simply because we have a nagging doubt about our capabilities to do it? If we know we can do most of it then we should recognise that there is support and guidance out there should we hit a tricky bit, but otherwise we should just go for it. That includes applying for a leadership position in the first place. When we look at the person specification for a job, unless it is in the essentials criteria, we should, like our toddlers just have a go! No leader is fully formed and 100% an exact fit for any organisation and so we should not assume we can't have a go at putting on the shoe just in case it doesn't fit; leadership roles are not a fairytale, the shoe doesn't need to fit exactly for the leadership recruitment story to have a happy ending.

The second learning point from our toddlers' struggles with footwear is the sheer determination and focus of our toddlers as they strive to master new skills, which is staggering. They shun other distractions, even bribery with promises of favourite treats if they'll just let you do it don't detract from their focus; they concentrate on the job in hand and are not drawn into extraneous noise or activity until their core work is done. And we as leaders can learn from this. We are all too often willing to let our own focus on a piece of work be eaten into by distraction. Sometimes this distraction is of our own making – an hour lost scrolling on social media or an overly long and inefficient fiddle about with the layout of a document. Sometimes, however, in a leadership role it is allowing others to distract us – dropping everything to be at everyone else's beck and call and to problem solve for everyone else. In leadership we need to model the wellbeing and efficiency strategies we would encourage across our organisation.

Being available to solve everyone's problems and drawing yourself away from your core work can be draining and inefficient as you are pulled away from your train of thought and so your actions and thinking becomes fragmented and even simple tasks take much longer than anticipated and your well-planned schedule goes to pot. Setting yourself up to be a superhero problem-solving leader does not develop independence in your organisation. Colleagues need to feel they have the autonomy and skills to make decisions without constantly seeking permission or reassurance and our own communications about our core work and associated procedures (our chocolate buttons and lollipops) needs to be clearly understood and embedded so that colleagues have a framework and points of reference to help inform their decision making without always having to pass things by us as the leader.

The more often we are pulled away from our core work by additional problems to solve – which are not actually part of our role and could actually have been resolved by a confident and skilled team – does not serve evidence that we are a great and talented and revered leader upon whom everything and everybody relies, but instead quite the opposite. The more we can empower our teams to solve problems and answer queries accurately and effectively without us is the true evidence of our effectiveness. Being needed is not the same as being an effective leader. Just as parenting a toddler who is learning to put their shoes on may initially seem frustrating and time consuming, soon they will have mastered it without us and will be able to do it in seconds, freeing us up to wonder where we've put the car keys!

In leadership we should be working towards creating autonomy, confidence and independence in our teams through effective identification of talent and skills alongside a provision of excellent professional learning and development opportunities. As with toddlers, as soon as there is more than one child, you simply don't have the time to be putting on everyone's shoes for them and they learn to do things very quickly when they don't have the luxury of their parent's undivided attention and time. This translates to teams too, the more independence is expected and modelled and culture of trust, support and shared values is created, the less likely you are to be pulled away from your leadership role to put on everyone's shoes for them. Just as in parenting the goal is effective, capable and confident independence for your children, so too it is leadership for your teams.

Questions to consider:
- How do we maintain focus on tasks? How good are we at managing distractions? Is our workspace conducive to uninterrupted periods of working and thinking? How might we adapt our working practices and communicate this to colleagues to reduce distraction and improve focus?
- How do I encourage independence, autonomy and professional confidence in colleagues? Are key messages about core work clear

and well understood so colleagues feel able to make decisions without consultation?

- How do I identify and nurture emerging talent in my organisation? What opportunities do I offer for staff at all levels to develop their own skills and knowledge?

4. Squirty bath taps and the breakfast disco: Find the fun

My eldest daughter, when she was just under two, discovered that if you put your hand under the bath tap when it was on you could direct a spray of water to soak anyone who happened to walk into the bathroom. I have a video of her belly laughing as she continually soaks the entire bathroom and me by squirting the water in my direction again and again. She's also one of the leaders of our almost daily 'breakfast disco' where we liven up a dull breakfast time by cranking up the music, singing and dancing away in highchairs and waving spoons to our favourite cheesy songs. This means that we often start and end the days squealing with laughter and have had some great time together as our little family team. There is not a day that passes which doesn't involve all of us cracking up with laughter at some point too. Toddlers are a constant source of hilarity and a reminder each day that there is something positive to think or to say or to do, which sadly, as adults, is a beautiful characteristic that seems to fade as the calendars' years pass by, and especially when we think of the role of a leader.

When you think of a great leader, I doubt you envisage that leader doubled over with laughter or cracking a joke. The historical narrative of successful leadership appears to be around dynamism, gravitas, confidence, consistency, sometimes charm or great intellect, but so very rarely positivity or humour. Try to think of ten famous effective leaders who you think have an excellent sense of humour or don't take themselves massively seriously or have an ego the size of a small elephant. Now list ten effective leaders who you think of as 'serious'. I am confident that the latter list is easier to populate than the first. But, why so?

Why is leadership seemingly synonymous with a lack of that most basic of human characteristics – a sense of humour? Maybe we as consumers of leadership are at fault, maybe we see laughter, humour and seeing things through a positive and light-hearted lens as being somehow childish, and that may be in part be because of the huge disparity between the number of times a day a child laughs and the number an adult laughs. But a positive outlook as a leader can be your biggest strength and can be what ensures that teams trust you, recognise your humility and humanity and through which you can build teams and get through the toughest of times as an organisation.

Now I am not saying we should enter a meeting dressed as a clown or be cracking jokes in a difficult HR conversation, but instead that as leaders we should radiate as much positivity as we can. As leaders we know we set the weather in our organisations. We are the mood barometer which everyone checks as they enter the building. If we are dour, snappy, disengaged or aloof then this will permeate through our teams and the work they do. If we are buoyant, positive and radiate energy and commitment then this is what helps to build the culture of our organisation. We want people to see us and reach for their sunglasses we are radiating that much light, not dashing for their umbrellas as we unleash today's tornado of negativity and pessimism. Now I am also not saying that, like a toddler, we should be guffawing every five minutes at the use of the word 'bum' or giggling uncontrollably if someone knocks something over, but we can bring a little lightness to all that we do. I have been in so many grey meetings over the years that were full of grey people in grey clothing talking about grey things, that left me feeling as if the Dementors from Harry Potter had just walked into the room and sucked out my soul.

Yes, as leaders our work is important and (dependent upon the context) can be life changing or have far-reaching financial or legal ramifications, but there is no need for us to take our lead from the demeanour of a funeral director. Being relatively young in my first leadership role at 26, where I was advising colleagues across my region who were over twice my age, meant that I was always worried about being seen as a young flibbertigibbet who had nothing to contribute, and so I dressed and I spoke with a gravity, seriousness and degree of formality which looking back I now realise made me look not entirely unlike my toddlers when they try on my shoes and drag my handbag around (which is my excuse for why I always lose my car keys).

Leadership does not have a uniform. It does not require you to leave your sense of humour at the door and neither does it require you to look down on anyone else in a meeting who tries to lighten the mood when the meeting content is as heavy and as dull as the anchor on a battleship. Humour is subjective, yes, but positivity and humanity are not. Wearing a mask to work where you are hiding behind a thin veneer of faux seriousness is exhausting. Professionalism is not about being grey. No one ever walked out of a grey style meeting feeling anything other than utterly drained and as if they had just been walloped with that anchor. Our job as leaders is to set the weather, so why do so many of us see leadership as the meteorological equivalent of November drizzle when in fact we could make it a dazzling summer sunset or a multi-coloured rainbow? You don't find our toddlers deciding that now they have mastered potty training and spoon feeding they need to don a smart suit and nod sagely at everyone whilst tapping away studiously at some new tech device or scribbling with a heavy and suitably expensive pen. Nope, they're off being themselves again and having their next adventure and laughing about it along the way and that is why people smile indulgently and warmly at toddlers when they're busy effecting toddler change and toddler learning and why conversely people sigh and visibly sag when they are called to leadership meetings.

You can simultaneously take your business seriously without being serious all the time but sadly the pervasive narrative around leadership seems to be predominantly about becoming like that anchor. However, true effectiveness as a leader is also all about light and shade or contrast.

There is no point leaping around like a children's TV presenter and playing practical jokes on staff or implementing toe-curlingly cringey 'fun' activities for staff to try and lighten the mood or present yourself as 'fun'. That kind of stuff only makes people want to engage with the back of their own eyelids and pray that it all ends soon so they can go home. Neither is it to create such a serious and corporate culture that everyone is forced to dredge up an Oscar-winning performances of the committed and dedicated uber-professional. We need to recognise that as leaders we lead people. People are messy and complicated and funny and diverse and ultimately unique. Yes, humour can be misconstrued and can cloud things when messages need to be crystal clear in terms of information or approach but it can also be deployed as a useful tool to share your own foibles and fallibility which is ultimately one way in which people will identify more with you as a leader. Setting the default to 'positive' will always ultimately reap more dividends than 'serious'. However, just as all great pieces of art or music require contrast and light and shade, so does your leadership.

Although the default setting may be positive, there are times where the chord change needs to shift from major to minor and you will need to flex your serious muscles. This then actually has a really positive and powerful effect because a deliberate employment of this for a specific situation means that people's attention will be drawn to the contrast and whatever you are trying to convey will be more likely to be heard as it is a contrast to your default setting. So, as leaders and in your leadership role, look for the equivalent of the squirty bath taps or the breakfast disco where you laugh and enjoy being with your teams. Humour is subjective but positivity is not and if you're having a drizzly anchor of a day, ensure that there is someone else you can trust in your team to present the leadership weather front for everyone until you've found your radiant sunset again.

5. Dinosaurs at the supermarket: Never worry what people think and do things your own way

All my children at some point have left the house dressed up as one of their favourite characters, but not for a fancy dress party. One of my favourite ones was with my youngest, my son who at one stage frequently went shopping in a full dinosaur outfit complete with giant foam dinosaur head. He had absolutely no self-consciousness about this decision and would simply roar at everyone and tell them that he was a T-Rex. Now how many of us as adults and leaders would have the confidence in our decision making to be as bold as this when presenting our stance to the world? In my son's eyes he was genuinely a dinosaur and there was nothing wrong at all about entering that wholeheartedly and in an utterly committed way. But how often as leaders do we just take the middle of the road route because we are afraid to do something a little different? We are afraid that our choices will be critiqued or mocked or will just plain fail but we need to think a little more deeply about what we are trying to do and who we are trying to please.

If we are trying to jump through the hoops of the small picture thinking and to just get things done and tick things off, then we are going to look pretty daft doing that dressed as earth's most ferocious prehistoric predator. However, if we are charting a new direction and setting a new strategic vision then that is definitely the time to cast off the shackles of mediocrity and assimilation and to roar with absolutely zero shits given. The courage of his conviction and the pride in his choice was something as leaders we need to hone. It goes back to our chocolate buttons and lollipops too: if we are absolutely clear about why we are doing something and what is important to us or our organisation, if it aligns with what we are trying to achieve and there is a clear rationale for doing it, then however ridiculous it may appear to those who are wallowing in that middle safe ground, we should be confident that we are in actual fact a T-Rex. Plus, being a T-Rex in a trolley at Tesco is nothing to raise an eyebrow at; it is something to celebrate.

Those of us who are nervous about our decisions are those who are on the cusp of doing something challenging. We are never nervous about the mundane or the expected or the usual; we get nervous when we are challenging ourselves or the system in which we work. Too often in teaching, schools and leaders do things to appease external accountability measures such as SATs results or Ofsted but this is dancing to the wrong drum. We spend hours producing documents and evidence where we're trying to prove that we're working rather than working to improve. This kind of 'busyness' and appeasement through focusing on the narrow accountability targets rather than the wider scope and reach of your actual work and its purpose is not being earth's most ferocious and confident predator, this is being a little scurrying egg collecting dinosaur (a 'Compsognathus', as my dinosaur obsessed three year old will tell you) and one who is fearful of all the other dinosaurs and also of being seen. If we spend the time ensuring our organisations are dominated by the external tick sheets of accountability rather than the wide-open landscape of possibility, then we are being far too Compsognathus and not enough T-Rex.

As leaders we need to develop the kind of belief in what we are doing and the choices we make that mean we can have the level of confidence in our actions of that of a toddler in a massive dinosaur head in the bread aisle in Tesco.

Questions to consider:
- Which projects are currently making you the most nervous? What is it about them that elicits this feeling (e.g. a lack of knowledge or experience, changing a long-established system or approach, doing something new and untested, having a challenging conversation or making an unpopular decision)? What are you currently doing to appease those nerves (e.g. seeking advice, researching alternatives, continued open dialogue and consultation)?
- How do current working projects align with the long-term bigger picture?

- Can we articulate why we are doing what we are doing in terms of our current projects? Can we see a purpose beyond initial accountability measures?
- How confident are we in our choices and decision-making around current projects?

Lesson four:
Tricky consistency

1. *I don't like Santa*: Don't be afraid to be unpopular

My middle daughter used to be terrified of Santa. Whilst other children would queue wide-eyed and full of the magic of the festive season to sit on Santa's lap and tell him their Christmas wishes, my daughter would scream so loudly it was as if the sledge had run over her foot. She would do anything to avoid Santa, so much so that one year she was so terrified he would be in her room to hang up her stocking that we had to go through some crazy rigmarole where hers and her elder sister's stockings weren't hung on the end of their beds but instead downstairs and also (upon her request) well away from the staircase.

One Christmas she even refused to open any presents because: 'Santa had touched them'. In fact, she was so adamant that we ended up recycling them and wrapping them in birthday paper for later in the year. She really hated the fella in red and most people, who obviously adored the whole Christmas and Santa thing, would meet that hatred with disbelief. However, despite how awkward it made family days out around Christmas time, (I don't know if you've ever tried to avoid pictures of Santa or people dressed as Santa during December but it's a bit like trying to avoid oxygen). We would round corners in shopping centres and be met by a charity Santa and we would greet him with a hysterical toddler running as if she were Usain Bolt in a remake of *The Great Escape*. We'd attend parties or pre-school events and whilst everyone else was misty-eyed with wonder, my daughter would be borderline banshee and bolting for the nearest exit. Despite her protestations, I couldn't help but admire how even with everyone telling her she was wrong and there was nothing to be scared of, she wasn't afraid to be unpopular and hold fast to her belief. In leadership we are often the fall guy, the one with whom the buck stops and where the ultimate accountability lies and with that comes the need to, on occasions, make unpopular decisions. But leadership is not a popularity contest. Sometimes in leadership you have to do what is right, not what is easy or popular. For this you need to reflect on a few things.

You need to ensure that you're clear about your chocolate buttons, your lollipops and your celery. You need to be resolute that you are doing the right thing because it aligns with your core values and vision. But that doesn't make things any easier. There will always be the bemused onlookers like with my daughter and Santa. There will always be people telling you that you are wrong like people who tried to convince my daughter, and there will be times – like she has now – when she realises that actually she might have been wrong and made the wrong decision. But when we have to make an unpopular decision we can only base it on the information we have at the time, alongside our own moral compass, and the needs and vision of what we are trying to create.

We also need to seek guidance if the unpopular decision is one which affects a person's life in terms of employment, pay, access to future employment/references, equality and discrimination, criminal activity or safeguarding and health and safety concerns. Some things require specialist guidance and we should never make a decision in these circumstances without first consulting about the legalities of the potential outcomes. Seeking advice in these situations is not a sign of a lack of knowledge or a weakness in leadership, it is a sign that although the decision may be unpopular, it was done with the latest specialist information and the most up-to-date guidance. In other situations, you may simply have to have a conversation that you find embarrassing, awkward or are afraid of because of potential volatility or a hostile reception. For these situations planning is key.

There are many great books out there which outline the exact ways in which you can structure the wording of these kinds of meetings, but my advice would simply be to plan, plan and plan again. Have every piece of evidence or information you need to hand and have rehearsed your calm and measured responses to any counters or accusations. If necessary, ensure that you have someone else to minute the conversation and never be afraid to call time on a meeting that is turning hostile or aggressive. You may be the fall guy, but you still deserve to be treated with decency. Also don't be afraid of silence or pauses during these meetings. With my daughter and Santa, I used to gabble apologies and a narrative of why she might be behaving like that in a constant nervous stream. In a challenging conversation, saying less often allows for clarity and processing time and can be a chance for both parties to reflect properly on what is being said and then what is *really* being said through non-verbal communication. My former co-head colleague is a master of using effective pauses and periods of quiet in challenging conversations. I have seen her defuse the most explosive of situations and also use silence as a comfort to those who may be confessing something to her in different situations. Sometimes as leaders we think we always need to know what to say in a challenging conversation, sometimes though we just need to start the conversation off and let the silence do a lot of the talking.

Once we accept that there are going to be difficult conversations to be had, we can also seek support before and afterwards for ourselves. Debriefing with a mentor, coach or trusted colleague is vital if we are to improve as leaders and help put things into perspective. What is not helpful is replaying the scene over and over at night in bed and worrying. Just as our toddlers would never agonise for hours over a squabble at the snack table or an altercation at the sand tray, we too need to develop the skills to separate what we could have done from what we actually did and then move on, either having learnt from it or having achieved the intended goal of the conversation.

Our challenging conversations should also always be done with positive regard and relationships at their core. If we invest in developing positive relationships with our staff and also with our stakeholders, then challenging conversations can be framed and conducted far more effectively. The halo effect means that we are much more likely to believe the information from someone we know, like or respect and are much less likely to believe those who we do not like and respect.

Investment in positive relationships with all stakeholders and staff will never be time wasted. You never know in leadership when you are going to have a difficult or challenging conversation. Having collateral in the 'relationships bank' can be hugely helpful when a need for one of these conversations arises. Investing in developing genuine and honest positive relationships throughout all that we do as a leader can mean we have a much greater understanding of an individual person and their situation/context before a difficult conversation, and a greater likelihood of the person, with whom you are talking to, receiving information more positively. This is not to say that we need to force false friendships. Even the youngest toddler can see through a fake smile or a disingenuous comment so we should not assume that we lose this skill as adults. Positive relationships are built on trust, mutual respect, consistency, fairness and the grossly underrated attribute of kindness. And in a world where you can be anything, be kind (especially if you have to have a challenging conversation).

2. *He's being mean to me!* Calling out negativity

If you parent a toddler, you will very quickly realise that a lot of your time is taken up with the concept of fairness or being mean. With three small children, I have often joked that my standard uniform should be the black shirt, shorts and whistle of a referee, such is the amount of time I spend attempting to sort out perceived injustices and accusations of foul play. I once saw a t-shirt on a website which bore the slogan, 'sibling referee' and although I was tempted to buy it, it was just the wrong side of irony and too close to the truth for it to be genuinely funny. I have sorted complaints of everything from who has the biggest piece of cake through to who gets the hallowed and single red cup in the house and caught many a tumbling child who is falling off the exact same chair their sibling is wedging themselves onto and which they both **must** have despite being in a room full of empty chairs.

The senses of injustice and fairness loom large in any interaction with toddlers; it is as if they are hardwired to call out anything that might necessitate co-operation or, dare I say it, sharing. As adults we are less likely to call out injustices. We are often so busy with our own day-to-day tasks that we either don't see, or feel we don't have the time or energy, to call out negativity. We are also often a sucker for a gossip or a vent and although sharing frustrations with a trusted colleague, friend, family member or mentor might actually be helpful for us; it is less likely to be helpful to let off a storm of rumbling gripes in the workplace.

As a leader you set the weather in your organisation. We have already spoken about how positivity and humour are often not aligned with professionalism in everyone's perception of leadership but remaining positive and also calling out negativity are actually key parts of leadership. That is not to say we should march into the staff room and berate weary workers on a Monday morning for not bounding around like Tigger, but that we should be vigilant to the gradual erosive consequences of negativity. The thing is, negativity is catching. If a person walks into a crowded staff meeting and begins to complain about something it is more than likely going to set off a chain reaction of domino grumbling. Once that domino stack is set off in its tumbling motion it can travel around the room like wildfire and all of a sudden the mood of the room is pessimistic and dour.

On occasions it may well be that everyone needs to have a bit of a moan; an unexpected photocopier breakdown can send even the most positive staff into a reprographics tailspin and you would expect there to be a communal sharing of woes as this is a one-off shared experience that has frustrated everyone and couldn't have been foreseen or necessarily prevented. However, if there is someone who, despite the lack of actual things to moan about, likes to pick fault and generally complain about everything then this is the time to call out negativity. By this I don't mean publicly calling them out, but rather through a conversation, asking if everything is OK and that you've noticed they often don't appear to be happy and is there anything you can do. I have often done this in leadership and more often than not, the unhappiness or dissatisfaction is either rooted in a perceived or unaddressed injustice in the workplace, which can then be explored and addressed, or that person struggling to cope with other demanding and competing pressures outside work.

It is important, therefore, as a leader, to build relationships and to be vigilant. Knowing your staff really well, understanding and taking an interest in their lives outside of work can be hugely illuminating when considering their attitudes at work. It may well be that one member of staff has an elderly parent who they have begun to care for who is adding additional hours to an already long day with their own families. It may be someone whose partner has been made redundant or someone who is coping with a sick child or a convoluted house move or relationship breakdown. Lives outside of work can either cast a shadow or a sunbeam across people's demeanour at work and we need to be both understanding and vigilant and then subsequently be there to offer or facilitate any appropriate support. However, if there were someone who was persistently and deliberately negative for no reason then this would need to be discussed.

Just as we would not accept our toddlers being in a persistently grumpy, unhelpful or obstinate mood without addressing things, so should we extend this same logic to our workplace. When someone is deliberately being toxic then we need to investigate the reasons why and draw the effects of their behaviour to their attention. We also need to act as champions of fairness when it comes to issues of inclusion, equality and equity. We need to ensure that we fully investigate and have robust systems for accusations of bullying, harassment and also for whistleblowing. We need to ensure that we facilitate everyone having a voice in decision-making, consultation and access to training, development and a safe and supportive working environment. We also need to consult widely across our wider systems to hear voices from organisations that may be more diverse than ours on issues relating to inclusion and equality. We must be aware of our own biases and seek to educate ourselves constantly about raising awareness of our own and potentially our organisation's biases. Our aim should be to have an organisation where, as Elly Chapple says, 'Everyone has a seat at the table', and should we find that, like our toddlers, someone is getting pushed off that chair, we need to ensure that we as the leaders take action.

3. *I don't want to play anymore*: Having difficult conversations

As adults we are significantly more tolerant in our day-to-day lives. There has been many a time I would have loved to have stood up in a meeting and announced that I was bored or hungry and therefore leaving. Imagine how liberating it would be, when you are tired or not feeling too great, to cancel evening plans with a simple, 'I don't want to'. It never ceases to amaze me how unburdened by social niceties our toddlers are and how they convey their feelings succinctly, without any grey areas, leaving any listener in no doubt as to their core message. Having an, 'I don't want to play anymore' conversation as a leader obviously needs to have less of this stinging lack of toddler tact, but we do need to take our clarity leads from them. How often have you left a meeting, especially one where there was a difference of opinion or a conflict and felt that somehow you were not heard or the conversation was derailed by superfluous detail or unrelated additional stories? More often than not this is because the meeting or conversation lacked that toddler clarity and focus.

When there is genuine disagreement or an issue that has rumbled on and needs resolution, focus and clarity are key. Toddlers state facts and this is what we need to focus on. They will simply say, 'Mummy, they're not sharing the blocks' or 'I'm sad because they hit me'. They don't add in apologies, rehashing previous incidents or give multiple excuses. The important thing in difficult conversations is to focus on facts and not be hoodwinked by extravagant and elaborate narratives or apologetic dulling comments. In many cases it is likely that there has been much informal support or dialogue prior to a tricky conversation and this has not been successful. It is also likely that the person involved has also had multiple opportunities to present their version of events and been involved in support, reminders or training to help address whatever issue requires resolution. It is at this point, where the usual open and supportive dialogue, practice and systems within the organisation have not worked and now the need to have a different kind of conversation presents itself. It is at this point that we need to remember what our toddlers did at this point. They came to seek adult support to tell them what had happened and to help navigate what to do next. This is exactly what we need to do as leaders in this situation.

When issues have arisen and there is a need to have a challenging conversation, we need to ensure we have consulted widely enough. Do we have all the facts? What events have led up to this point? Have we re-read any associated policies? Have we consulted HR, if necessary? Have we talked it through with experienced colleagues or specialists? Are we aware of any contributory or mitigating factors? Have we got all dates, times, names correct? Have all attendees been briefed? Are we aware of any additional attendees such as chaperones, professional representation or support? Have we collated any evidence that is required, such as photographs, testimonies, screenshots, emails, and so on. Have we drawn a timeline of events and collated all information? The better we are prepared for these challenging conversations the better.

Once we have collated all the information, are we sure of what we intend the meeting outcome to be? Have we got absolute clarity on what we will say and what the potential outcomes could be? Have we allowed time either side of the meeting for all attendees to prepare and reflect? It is worth noting that these sorts of meetings should ideally be held when the people involved do not have to go directly back to work, especially if the meeting may be particularly complex or emotive; conversely neither is a Friday afternoon usually ideal as there will be the weekend where nothing can be actioned or followed up. Unlike our toddlers, we do need to document what was said and agreed during these sorts of conversation. Deciding on mutually agreed actions for all parties is the main goal and so following up promptly with minutes or feedback is also key so that everyone has an accurate record of what was said and agreed.

Tricky conversations are inevitable in leadership and they are never any leaders favourite part of the job. How we approach them should be pragmatic but also kind. The kindness we continue to demonstrate and confer to others even when we are in a challenging situation will say more about us as leaders than anything else. When the chips are down and the stakes are high, those leaders who can still convey kindness and humanity whilst maintaining clarity are those who will ultimately be more successful; tricky conversations, although dealing with conflict, need not be adversarial.

4. I'm not going to put on my shoe

My first child was a breeze in terms of behaviour. They may have pretty much never slept a wink at night until they were almost two-and-a-half years old, but they made up for it in near perfect behaviour during the day. As I looked on at other parents dealing with endless tantrums, screaming and limb thrashing miniature whirlwinds in supermarket aisles, and absolute refusal to put on coats or sit down at the table, my eldest child neatly slotted into the mould of 'practically perfect in every way'. I put this down to a combination of many years of teaching experience and child psychology qualifications meaning that, of course, it was all down to parenting and expectations.

And then I had a second one.

And I had to gorge on my own words and eat a shedload of humble pie. With my first it was simply luck.

My second child is a tiny little fighter. She was born early and had hung on during a very difficult pregnancy. This tenacious character developed in toddlerhood into admirable obstinacy and a staggering degree of determination. My first ever glimpse of this was when she was about 18 months old and we were due at my mother-in-law's for tea. I asked my middle daughter to bring me her shoes from her bedroom onto the landing so I could put them on for her after I'd helped my eldest with the buckles on hers. I was met with a resounding, 'no'.

I wasn't going to give in so I repeated my instructions cheerily and at regular intervals every minute or so whilst my eldest daughter and I read books and played on the landing. Time passed and soon she had been in a furious glowering stance for almost half an hour. She hadn't cried nor had she moaned, she was just absolutely determined that bringing me those shoes was not for her. I have never seen a look quite like it on anyone's face nor seen a more powerful quiet display of 'no' in my life. She didn't scream or engage in argument, she simply dug her little shoeless heels in and refused to budge. It was a superb lesson in the power of no.

The trouble with so many of us as leaders is that we are wary of saying no. We end up taking on so much that it clouds our vision, clogs up our diaries and we end up chasing our tails and becoming utterly exhausted. My middle daughter's power of no extended to pretty much everything once she had made her mind up. What fascinated me though was her focus when she was trying to master something new. She would become totally engrossed and focused on one skill or task and would not stop until she had mastered it. Bribes, attempted distractions and offers of help would all be brushed off until she had completed her important work. This meant she became very good at a lot of things at a very young age and often much earlier than her elder sister. I remember her coming in to see me wearing a pair of tights she had put on herself perfectly at not much over a year old. If you've ever tried putting tights on a baby who's wearing a nappy you'll know this is no mean feat.

This utter focus on getting things right is something we can all learn from. She had picked an action or a skill she really wanted to hone and nothing was going to distract her. How often do we grant this extended and complete focus to a project in our organisations or on developing ourselves? We all too often flit from idea to idea, partially rolling out the latest 'next big thing' without giving adequate attention or focus to what we are already trying to achieve. Saying 'no' and developing a culture where projects are seen through and a focus is on doing things well – rather than on doing lots of things – is championed is likely to bear more fruit than that scattergun approach, which is the toddler equivalent of dumping everything out of the toybox in one go and then wondering why you can't piece together the jigsaw. Developing organisations and the people in them takes time, commitment and focus. We often associate commitment with the word 'yes' as this is the positive aspect of agreeing to commit to something but the other side of commitment is the word 'no'.

By harnessing the power of no we enable a minimising of distraction and a ring fencing of focus. Being able to say no as a leader is just as much about leadership strength. A yes requires capacity and too many yeses and not enough capacity will ultimately end up sinking the ship. A 'no' ensures that resources are focused, adequate time is allocated and there is clarity around what is important.

Lesson five: Maintaining wellbeing in a leadership role

1. Prioritising the basics: Sleep, food and play

I have spent a disproportionate amount of time over the last nine years trying to persuade my babies to sleep. I have bought every gadget, gizmo and book on how to cajole your miniature insomniac into bed and off to dreamland at a reasonable hour. If you ever meet me, you'll see that the dark circles under my eyes and my abundant wrinkles are the bedtime battle scars of a sleep time soldier defeated by a tiny army of sleep thieves. However, I also have noticed over those nine years another trend in that when they were tired and wanting to sleep, they actually slept! The simple need for sleep was never ignored, it was just massively inconvenient that my children appeared to exist in a different hemisphere to me and, therefore, wanted to sleep all day and be awake all night.

Once they were toddlers and actually sleeping at night (yes, there was not a single baby in this house who did a full night's sleep before their second birthday; how I'm not sitting in a wicker bath chair covered in a checked blanket in a sanctuary for the chronically sleep deprived I do not know) then I noticed that they would actively prioritise sleep. They would tell me if they were tired and my youngest has the most delightful and endearing habit of almost daily at some point standing up, sighing and announcing, 'I'm off for a rest'. He'll then lie in his bed and just either stare at the ceiling and cuddle one of his soft toys and basically chill out a bit until he's ready to re-join the playing. It always makes me smile that he is so in tune with his need for a rest and has no qualms about prioritising his need for a bit of downtime and a bit of peace and quiet. He's also the first one to be in a massive grumpy mood if breakfast is not on the table the moment he gets downstairs. In fact, I now prepare the breakfast before I even get him up, so 'hangry' can that boy get.

Once fed, he's a delight again and then spends the day punctuating it with various repeated requests for snacks and queries about when is it dinnertime. In fact, his sisters are also seemingly constantly hungry. You would think I lived in a house where Old Mother Hubbard had been the inspiration for our provision of food; such are the combined exaggerated protestations of hunger. If I added together all the hours I'd spent preparing snacks and miniature meals then I'm fairly sure I could have accrued enough to do a doctorate or train for a marathon or another such time-intensive hobby. Instead, I have spent many hours chopping up cubes of cheese and cucumber and trying to wrench packets of snaffled crispy bears out of fingers five minutes before it's lunchtime. What is interesting though is that you'll rarely see a child skip a meal or feign that they're not hungry when in fact they're ravenous, just because they have something they need to do.

If a toddler's tummy is rumbling then they seek to do something about it and you won't find them pressing on through a mountain of block stacking, xylophone bashing or doll tending when they're hungry and their stomach is growling. Toddlers are always first to meet their basic needs. Wrestling them through a fractious bedtime and bathtime where they protest they are 'not tired' is often part of the ritual of parenting but once in their pyjamas and in their beds, most of the time they're fast asleep. Toddlers will always ensure their basic needs are met, this is one of the reasons they are learning machines as well as having boundless energy – oh *so* much energy! As adults we are too often careless and profligate with attending to our basic needs. We forget that we are humans first and need to prioritise self-care and basic elements of health like good sleep hygiene and a nutritious diet. Ironically, when we need our sleep and decent fuel the most, when times are busy or challenging, this is when we put ourselves under the most pressure. We skip meals, we don't exercise, and we don't get enough sleep by either working late into the night or suffering from the dreaded insomnia. And it is often a vicious cycle. We are tired so we rely on highly-caffeinated drinks, junk food and sugar, which subsequently makes us more wired and less able to switch off.

It is well known that sleep deprivation makes us crave unhealthy foods and so we enter into a destructive cycle of tiredness, dehydration, over-indulging in caffeine and sugar crashes. Now I'm not going to tell you to batch cook brown pasta and eight vegetable sauces from scratch, I'm a sucker for a doughnut and live on Diet Coke. Nonetheless, I do know that I feel better when I put in the effort to eat properly, regularly and to not rely on stimulants to get me through the day. I also know that when I'm tired I am rubbish at home and pretty average at work. Being tired clouds our judgement and makes us more likely to react negatively or over emotionally. Anyone who has dealt with an insomniac newborn for weeks on end will tell you of the real and genuine physical and mental effects that chronic sleep deprivation has. Your memory is affected, your moods are unpredictable and you are a shadow of your usual self. The restorative and levelling power of sleep should never be underestimated and yet it is one of the first things we cut when we are feeling under pressure.

Pushing yourself to carry on with limited sleep through a period of intense pressure is like flying a plane through bad weather and then deciding the thing to do is to remove one of the engines. It's only going to end badly if we do not prioritise sleep. When we are charged with making reliable, well-informed and thoughtful decisions in our daily work as leaders, the last thing we need to do is to enter into those decisions not firing on all cylinders. On occasions there will be a pinch point in the diary or a sudden emergency or accountability/inspection period at work where our sleep may be affected, but these associated longer days and shorter nights should only ever be the exception not the norm.

There is a reason why the phrase 'let's sleep on it' has endured, because sleep affords us the opportunity of restorative reflection, rest and reasoning. Things genuinely do look brighter in the morning, unless that morning comes after only a couple of hours of shut-eye. We also need to be mindful and vigilant as to how much rest our staff are getting. If we are constantly modelling a presenteeism attitude of permanent dedication and subsequent exhaustion then this is the message about workplace behaviours we are sending to our staff. Exhaustion and sleep deprivation are cruel mistresses and it would be a foolish leader who let these creep up on their staff and wreak havoc with sickness, periods of absence and ability to carry out tasks effectively. We should never underestimate how much of an effect our own behaviours and attitudes have on the actions of our staff. Even if we do not articulate it, getting in first and leaving last and working late into the night each evening will set the tone for the working culture in our organisations.

There is much evidence about how efficiencies drop off after over 50 working hours and so we should be proactive in modelling efficient, healthy and effective working habits, which encourage our staff to prioritise their basic health and wellbeing needs. Lunchtime meetings, not taking regular breaks, skipping meals are all noticed by our staff and we need to model how being effective does not equate with failing to eat, rest, sleep or exercise. It is interesting to note that over the academic year of 38 weeks, taking just a 30-minute lunch break every day would equate to an additional 10-12 full working days off; imagine how much better you would feel if you had an additional 12 days off! If we want our staff to be efficient and effective and to feel appreciated, we need to encourage them to prioritise their own health and wellbeing. There needs to be the avoidance of the pervasive culture of presenteeism.

For some people, working late into the evenings during the week or for a few days per week helps them to ring fence family time at home and at weekends. For others they may like to leave early each day to see children or to pursue a hobby or study and may well choose to complete some tasks later in the evening. The point is that there is not a one size fits all model to working patterns, but the overall message should be that done is all that matters; when you choose to do it and fit it around what works for you is actually best. Trying to prove you are working and dedicated by being first in, last out and then taking work home constantly sends the message that others should be doing this too and this message can be corrosive and damaging.

Of course, there are always busy points within a year for an organisation and times when it's all hands on deck and extra hours need to be pulled in, but this should be balanced with periods of relative calm and quiet. There should be an ebb and flow to the year within an organisation and therefore people should not be attempting to sprint at full speed 365 days a year, when a gentle jog would still get the job of work done whilst retaining those energy reserves for the busier times.

If we look at our work as leaders, we also spend a disproportionate amount of our time sitting. We go from meeting to meeting where for a long period of time we are often sat around a table with copious amounts of tea and coffee and usually a plate of biscuits in front of us. If we are on our feet it is often only for short periods and the rise in the popularity of fitness trackers and step counters has brought into the public gaze just how sedentary many people are. Just the associated workplace attire of leadership is often not conducive to movement; ties, footwear, tailored clothing, jackets, belts, and so on. No one goes home and decides to change into something more comfortable by selecting a suit, shirt and formal footwear. We are often constrained not only by our clothing choices but also the structures of our days, yet physical movement is so important to our overall health and wellbeing.

If you observe a toddler, they are very rarely still. Even when they are concentrating on playing, they will be in a deep squat or lying on their stomachs. They have beautiful posture and delight in running, jumping and the release of physical movement. Indeed, rainy days with a toddler are why so many parents find themselves in that circle of hell that is called 'soft play', as toddlers need that physical movement and exertion as part of their everyday lives. A rainy day to them does not mean a Netflix binge and taking it easy. There is no rest day for toddlers; they are movement machines! We need to emulate this as it also contributes to our ability to sleep well and function more effectively.

We only have one body and choosing not to look after our cardiovascular system, our muscle mass and our general flexibility and stamina is only storing up trouble. I am not one of those people who is devoted to sports, who tackles half marathons or takes part in military style mud runs or staggeringly long bike rides. Neither am I a yoga devotee or advocate of Pilates, but I do love going to the gym. It is a time for me to exert myself in a way different to the mental exertion of work or the emotional exertion of parenthood. I am able to focus on a different aspect of my wellbeing and it also gives me a chance to think and to reflect on my own whilst listening to podcasts or my favourite music. When I miss a session or two during the week, I notice the dip in my mood or my energy. When we feel tired, we don't want to exercise but this is rarely a tiredness from actual physical exertion, it is the numbing tiredness of lack of sleep or overworking. Physical tiredness ensures our sleep is deeper and that our bodies remain fit enough to cope with the demands in the rest of our lives.

As leaders, how often do we prioritise this for ourselves and how often do we just collapse at the end of a day, especially if you have the 'second job' of a young family or a caring commitment when you return from work? If we are to be learning machines like toddlers and full of the energy to lead and to maintain our leadership stamina, we need to watch and learn from our toddlers. We need to prioritise the toddler basics of sleep, food and play – rest, diet and exercise.

2. The monster under the bed: Seeking support when things are scary

Once you get through the chaos that is multiple wake ups per night with a baby, you have the nocturnal delights of nightmares. Just when you think it's safe to say you might just have an uninterrupted night just your head on your pillow dreaming of a small libation on a deserted beach you are awoken either by a blood curdling scream or, even more terrifying, a tiny face pressed right up to yours in the pitch black, which scares the wotsits out of you.

Once your own heart rate has dropped a few dozen beats per minute and you've established that there isn't actually a need to employ your best made up kung fu moves to ward off a midnight intruder, you realise that your toddler has simply had a nightmare. Sometimes it is a genuine nightmare they have had and you gather them up, their little trembling bodies, shaking with real fear, and you comfort and reassure them that all is well and there is nothing to worry about. Other times they are just a bit fed up in the night and fancy a bit of company, which is fine, but you'd really rather they didn't choose two in the morning to decide that now is the time for a catch up.

What fascinates me about toddlers and nightmares though is their ability to seek immediate support. You don't find toddlers who are deciding they won't tell anyone about their nightmare and they'll try and work it out for themselves and just get on with things. You don't find a toddler trying to cover up that they've had a nightmare; they're straight to you, seeking support, reassurance and guidance. Now in leadership we need to do exactly the same when we discover a monster under the bed. When things go wrong, as they invariably do at some point, there will be moments of leadership that are actually truly terrifying. This may be dealing with the death of a colleague or in schools of a child. It may be an accusation of a perceived wrongdoing, or it may be not achieving the expected outcome in one of your accountability measures.

Either way, we will all experience the shock, terror and bewilderment of being utterly out of our depths at some point and if we try to navigate these periods alone, we will soon find we are drowning. That is why it is imperative that we have trusted people to support us who are outside our organisations. Whether these be trained mentors or coaches, former colleagues, colleagues in similar roles in other organisations, union representatives or simply our own partners or family, we all need someone to help steer us through the stormier times.

When you start in a leadership role, every day is a new day until you've done your first year. You will be assimilating everything from the rhythm of the year right through to the attitudes and aptitudes of your staff and the measurable outcomes and data. This is enough in itself to be challenging and I would advise anyone taking on a new leadership position to ensure they have someone who is experienced in the sector to act as a guide and mentor. We also need to have someone to whom we can turn when the unexpected or shocking happens. Developing a trusted network of a balance of experts alongside people who know you well and love you are vital as a team to call on when the proverbial hits the fan. When bad things happen though, just as our toddlers we need to be proactive in seeking support; whether it be a genuine screaming nightmare or just the need for a chat and a bit of reassurance, we too need to find someone to help tuck us back into our role and either help us to brave the night or just be there for company. Leadership can be a lonely role, especially if you are the one right at the top of the organisation. Ensuring we have adequate support systems that we can call on when times get scary will ensure that we don't end up having a complete leadership nightmare.

Questions to consider:
- Who do we have in our support networks to support us in/as:
  Areas of the role in which we are unsure or inexperienced
  General leadership advice
  Experts in specific areas to inspire, counsel and guide

A trusted confidante to share concerns or worries

Colleagues in similar settings to share best practice

A coach or mentoring specialist

- How comfortable are we at seeking support?
- How often do we 'take stock' of what is on our plates and look to seek guidance or to delegate?
- How often do we seek to widen our professional networks to both offer and to broaden our network of potential support?

3. *She's my best friend now!* Grudges are a waste of time

Toddlers are fickle, or maybe they're just more forgiving. Either way it never ceases to amaze me how they can go from fighting like cat and dog to giggling together conspiratorially in the playhouse in moments. Their ability to not hold a grudge or to remain in a grumpy mood is a skill we all need to hone. Despite the often-ear-splitting squealing and the associated fury of a sibling squabble, I can often come between the two warring factions as they stare, tense-jawed and puce with rage, whilst they articulate their misdemeanours. Then, in a heartbeat, they're best buddies and laughing like nothing at all happened whilst I am still stood there utterly bemused in full referee mode.

It is this ability to forgive, to move on and to not dwell on things that we as leaders need to improve on. When someone unsettles things either by repeatedly letting us down, by being actively and negatively disruptive at work or who continually doesn't complete the job of work for which they are paid, it can be easy to let seething resentment overtake and cloud all of our judgements and our mood for the remainder of the day. I'm not saying that we should develop a permissive attitude where underperformance and lackadaisical attitudes are the order of the day, but that instead we need to become skilled at compartmentalising our responses to individual events during the day so they do not cast a long and gloomy shadow over the rest of our decision-making and interactions.

There will always be people in an organisation who – despite our best efforts – are infuriatingly disruptive, unwilling to engage, who underperform or continually sell the organisation short in terms of their output and effort. There will be, in contrast to this, scores of others who are engaged, wholeheartedly positive, helpful, highly skilled and exceptionally effective in all they do. Sadly in leadership, our role as part of the organisation's accountability structure means that often it is us who are on the front line of tackling those in the former group. Addressing negativity, disengagement, underperformance or misconduct is immensely time consuming, often messy and convoluted, and depletes your emotional and mental reserves very quickly.

Cases can rumble on almost interminably, producing acres of trees worth of paper trails and we can easily become obsessed with every small detail and nuance of the case, beginning to lose objectivity and take it personally, and worse still, letting it skew our view of what could be a very positive vista across the rest of our organisation. Being the person with whom the buck stops can mean that you often have to deal with things which are uncomfortable, volatile and frequently utterly infuriating but it is how much conscious effort we put into ensuring we don't dwell unconsciously on the negativity of each of these situations that will ensure we can move on and be skipping off to the more restorative and positive sides of our role.

Ensuring there is time to debrief following a meeting with a trusted colleague or mentor is useful in ensuring any stormy feelings are not thundered into our next task. All parents know that feeling of exasperation at home when our toddlers knock over their full bowl of cereal onto the kitchen floor, the cat brings in a dead pigeon and then the baby decides to be sick all down their clean sleepsuit that you just put them in. It would be easy to let the utter frustration (and if I'm honest, sleep-deprived snivelling) transfer into the rest of the day, but taking time to take stock, reassess and then press on is the order of the day.

I'll never forget a particularly testing afternoon when my middle daughter was in an especially trying mood; my eldest was competing in the grumpy Olympics and currently on for a gold medal and my youngest had spent the afternoon wailing at top volume for no apparent reason. I had cooked a dinner for everyone, which apparently was akin to trying to poison them all such was the level of protestation, and then from nowhere, a massive swarm of bees flew through the open window of the kitchen and all hell broke loose. It was utter bedlam and in the chaos and panic of herding three children upstairs and away from the swarm (which was on the move from an unknown and previously unseen nest in the eaves) the bad moods of everyone were forgotten. It was also similar to the time I'd got all three of them undressed in the girls' bedroom whilst the bath was running and my middle child shut the bedroom door but the handle came off in her hand. We were all locked in the bedroom with a running bath, the key in the front door downstairs, no one with a spare key to the house, my phone in the other room and all the kids completely naked. All I needed was a vicar to jump out of the wardrobe with a feather duster and I'd have had a French farce.

It would have been easy to have spent the rest of those chaotic days where everyone and everything was going wrong bemoaning my lack of luck and deciding that the best way to address the rest of the day would be through grumbling, griping and sullenly proclaiming parenting and my entire life to be a shambles as I was obviously not coping and my kids hated me for my ineptitude. As it was, both situations were eventually hilarious and involved much ingenious on the spot problem solving and a race against time before we flooded the bathroom and filled the kitchen below with soapy tepid toddler bathwater. Especially in those relentless November rainy days where the kids are utterly bored stiff as you can't go outside and play and you've exhausted all play dough, CBeebies and book reading options a million times over, you need a regular check in with your internal grump barometer. One way I coped with having three small children, and a life that appeared to resemble a badly written slapstick sitcom, was to seek help and support from other parents. The knowledge that they too had similar kinds of days and could offer advice on everything from potty training, weaning and occasionally just raising a toast to surviving another day was often enough to lift my mood and also to give genuine and useful support and advice for navigating some of the parenting bumps in the road I hit. Knowing I was not alone in the chaos of three small children meant that I was more able to focus on the positive and often the humorous and not be ground down by the more wearing aspects alongside the moments of chaotic maelstrom which frequently punctuate the parenting of small people.

And at the end of each day, when bedtime was finally sorted and the house had been rid of flooding baths, swarms of bees and everyone was safely gathered in, I often used to mentally thank my support network for getting me through another day. Now there was just the nocturnal drama to deal with! And it is the same in leadership. When things are going seemingly really dismally or someone is constantly making the workplace unpleasant and unproductive, we need to work hard to maintain objectivity and remember that we can't hold a grudge against our entire approach to our roles just because of one scenario or one person. In the same way that a toddler can compartmentalise what goes on in a sibling spat and then move seamlessly into the next fun-filled playtime, without constantly chewing over the sour curd of a dreadful meeting or a tedious task, so too should we attempt to box off those elements which cause our jaws to clench and our eyelids to twitch.

Effective leaders don't hold grudges or dwell too long on what could have been. Effective leaders will be straight back into the playhouse of their organisation after dealing with something tricky, often restored by a sneaky snack on their leadership chocolate buttons – guaranteed to provide a timely reminder that if you're holding onto those, it's always a good day and you'll have made the right decision.

4. Puddle jumping: Maintaining a connection with the outdoors for overall wellbeing

If you look in the porch cupboard in our house you'll find dozens of tiny wellies, waterproofs, umbrellas and hats. Since they were very tiny we've always been up, out the door and into whatever weather the day has thrown at us in order to get our fix of fresh air. There is no weather too extreme for us to venture out. We've been out in the garden in an unexpected snowstorm at six in the morning. We've gone for a walk in wind so strong it actually blew my middle child off her feet and into a hedge where she emerged, covered in bits of twig and leaves, to an elder sister who could barely breathe for laughing. We have jumped in puddles in rainstorms and once on holiday in an absolute deluge, they stripped naked and danced on the holiday accommodation veranda, laughing hysterically and banging on the patio windows with glee.

We've been on bike rides in temperatures well below zero; deliberately gone out puddle jumping in lashing rain; and, always, always, *always* go for a long walk at some point every day, regardless of what the weather is. I'm not going to lie – I don't always enjoy it. I'm much more of a fair weather walker and love curling up on the settee with a cup of tea and a remote control, but there is something genuinely special about a daily walk where you notice the subtle changes of the seasons, the different tastes and temperatures of the air, and then the warm return to a toasty home that makes all the difference to your motivation, your mood and your ability to deal with the day. It's also a reminder of the need to vary the pace and notice the small stuff. Walking with small children takes ten times longer than a normal walk. Every small item from a daisy to a snail to a discarded cigarette butt has to be inspected with rapt attention and wonder. This slowing down and being outdoors is balm for the leadership soul.

In the often frenetic pace of leadership decision-making and the weight of responsibility, a meander outside can do wonders for our overall health and wellbeing, as well as bringing us a huge dollop of perspective in terms of reminding us that there is literally a big wide world outside of our leadership world of work.

Leadership roles also often mean that we spend a disproportionate amount of time in small, confined rooms full of people and paper or we are alone in our cars travelling to another of said meetings. When we think of a leader we do not necessarily think of someone being outdoors but being outside is so important for our wellbeing and health. In the dark winter months when the snooze of the alarm rudely chides us for not immediately leaping up to greet the dark of another early morning, we haul ourselves into work often before the sun is up. As we get back into our cars at the end of a day, we often realise we haven't seen daylight all day. It is as if we live in a darkened underground world where the only lights we see are the blue glows of our devices and the harsh artificial office lighting of our organisations. Is it any wonder then that we are prone to often feeling drained, tired and lacking in motivation. If we are to feel refreshed in our leadership roles we need to reconnect with the wider world and the outdoors. Whether this is a stroll with the dog, a run, a brisk walk to the shops or simply sitting outside in the fresh air we need to ensure that we do not live our lives solely in the small airless worlds of our offices. Just as our toddlers crave the freedom and stimulation of being outdoors with all of its natural wonders and distractions, so too should we actively ring fence time in our schedules for coming out of our four walls and enjoying a little puddle jumping; I would just advise against the naked patio dancing in the rain!

5. Go away!

Our children are often brutal in their requests. The niceties of polite society or the unwritten rules of not hurting anyone else's feelings do not shackle them. I watch sometimes with horror the way in which they articulate what to them is a perfectly reasonable response or request, but should it have been uttered by an adult would have them shunned for their bluntness or lack of social grace. However I am secretly envious of one thing that toddlers say and do. They frequently say 'go away', often accompanied by the angry flourish of a lobbed building block. They have no qualms in telling anyone, adult or child, to simply leave them alone and I often find myself wishing I had that level of directness! They deliberately and without hesitation ask people to simply give them some time and space. Sometimes this is so that they can enjoy playing by themselves with a toy or book and other times it is because they don't like the person pulling on their time and attention. As leaders (and often leaders who are juggling family commitments), the chunk of time we often sacrifice first on the altar of busyness is that in which we had organised to do something for ourselves. This might be an evening out with friends, a hobby, an exercise class, a visit to the gym, shopping or simply binge-watching TV in our dressing gowns. We are so quick to deny ourselves the chance to do something we like in leadership and we then wonder why we feel depleted or frustrated or snappy.

As humans we simply cannot be 'on' all the time and we also cannot devote all of our time – every moment of every day – to pleasing other people. Ring fencing time for us to do what we want to do (including saying no to friends and family) and ensuring we get time to do what we enjoy means that we then give more freely to our families and our work without the bubbling resentment of self inflicted and unwilling martyrdom. Having time away from family and from work gives us time to think about nothing and this is important. We need time and space in which to let off cognitive or physical steam and to immerse ourselves in something that we love doing or simply the love of doing nothing. Great leaders need time for inspiration to strike too and if we are constantly playing whack-a-rat with our diaries and never affording ourselves the opportunity to stand back and enjoy something then we will soon burn out or begin to feel frustrated and unfulfilled.

Having time for yourself is not selfish. We would not expect those we care about or that we work with to be 'on' and available 24/7, neither would we expect them to have nothing to talk about which inspired or excited them. Pursuing things we enjoy and having time just to ourselves means that we can bring balance, clarity and a sense of personality to all that we do both at home and at school. The old saying that 'all work and no play makes Jack a dull boy' could be updated to say 'all work and no play and then leisure time filled with stuff he also doesn't want to do makes Jack not only dull but mightily fed up'. So developing our confidence to simply say 'go away' will help enormously with our efficiencies, both at home and at work. It might be best not to chuck a Duplo brick when you say it though.

6. 'Dogdog' and big sisters

My middle daughter has a fluffy toy dog that was gifted to me when I was pregnant with her. A wonderful former colleague gave me the dog, and it was one amongst dozens of similar stuffed animals and comfort blankets which we were given by generous family and friends. Almost six years on and that same toy dog which was once almost white, fluffy and rotund is now almost flat, worn nearly bare in places and is a dubious shade of beige. But Dogdog, as he is now known, is probably one of the most loved scraps of any material on the planet. Dogdog has endured everything from technicolour sick, to tears and snot, to being hurled down slides, had his ears repeated twiddled and his tail wiggled non stop whilst my daughter clasps him to her face with her thumb jammed in her mouth.

Dogdog is the first thing my daughter reaches for when she is sad, scared or nervous. He has travelled the globe with us and is never more than a few feet from her. We once lost him somewhere at nanny and grandad's house where he was missing for six long and tearful weeks until my mum found him. He had slipped beneath the lining of a trolley bag which the children had been playing with and was only discovered when the bag wouldn't fold into the boot of my mum's car as poor Dogdog was jammed in the lining near the hinges. Never in the history of homecomings has there been more joy or delight etched onto a face as on that of my daughter when her beloved Dogdog was returned. Everyone who knows her knows that he is special. When she attended playgroup he sat slumped and mournful but on guard on a special shelf in the playgroup hall as she played and tentatively began to make new friends. All of the neighbours and every keyworker she ever had at nursery or playgroup always says hello to not only my daughter but also Dogdog whenever we're out and about. He's the most photographed fleecy hound in the world too as he's in pretty much every family photo we've every taken.

The gradual degeneration of his appearance correlates exactly with the years passed in the pictures and the amount of sheer love he's had poured into him. He's the last thing she gives me before she trots out of the house and off to school in the mornings and the first thing she asks for when I pick her up. I have to wash him sneakily and surreptitiously as Dogdog is always a little on the unsavoury side when it comes to fragrance, but my daughter doesn't care. To her, he is the most perfect friend in the universe and she always feels better when her best friend is by her side. The day she started at big school age four, she broke my heart.

After the usual morning rush to get all three of them dressed, ready and out the door with the correct shoes on and no one wearing their breakfast as face art, I returned home after school drop off and nipped upstairs to check the bedrooms were tidy and that is when I saw Dogdog and burst into tears. He was in her bed, her beautifully made bed that she had made extra smart and neat now she was a 'big girl who goes to big school', and there he was, tucked under the smoothed duvet with his head on her pillow and his paws resting over the top. She really loved that toy dog and, when I picked her up, I asked her why he was tucked inside and not on her bed. She told me that she thought he would be lonely without her so she'd tucked him up in her bed so he could dream about her until she got home to cuddle him again. And we all need a Dogdog in our lives and especially in leadership. We all need the support and unconditional love for at least one person who will make us feel as brave, independent and as cared for as Dogdog does for my daughter.

When we get home after a long or difficult day, we need someone who will, without words, just as Dogdog, know exactly how to make us feel better. This may be a partner, a friend, a child, a parent, or your own real life living dog or cat, but we all need someone to make us feel the calm and serenity as an antidote to the chaotic world out there that my daughter has with her Dogdog. We should never underestimate also the fact that it is often hard to live with a leader, to watch the person you love frequently give the best of themselves to others during their daily working lives and then return depleted and shadowy with just a few leftovers for the ones they love. We need to be aware that our relationships with those we love need to be as reciprocal as those of my daughter and Dogdog. She takes him on adventures; he's by her side in everything she does from playtime and family meals out to simply just being together and doing nothing. In return he supports and reassures her and together they present a united little front. Although we need to find our Dogdog to travel with us as we pursue our passions, we also need to be mindful that we would never want our most loved and cherished real life Dogdogs to sit downstairs alone as we type or work late into the night or forget to ask them how they're feeling as we're so consumed with the messy business of the day at work. Although we may be deeply passionate about our leadership work, we must never want them to think, 'I wish I had been your passion'.

Ideally you'll also have a Dogdog at work; I don't mean a literal stuffed animal that you whip out when you're feeling wobbly but an actual genuine friend at work, someone who knows you as a person not just a leader. I was lucky enough to jobshare with a colleague who is now one of my best friends in the world and is actually my middle daughter (and therefore Dogdog's) godmother. On the days when life or leadership were truly awful, she was always there to either laugh, advise or help coach me through things. I trusted her as a colleague completely and wholeheartedly and when we were together I felt as if we could tackle anything. In leadership it can often be so lonely as there is no one doing the same job with the same huge responsibility as you but finding your Dogdog can be a key part in being able to be effective.

You don't have to have a best friend at work; you may work with people with whom you have absolutely zero in common and would never choose to socialise with but there will always be one person with whom you can have a really supportive and trusted genuine connection. When you have a work Dogdog then you know you have someone you trust to discuss things with and who you know is on your team, especially when you are having to make difficult or unpopular decisions. I have always been lucky enough to find at least one person in all of my workplaces who has become my Dogdog, and having someone at every career stage to help you through the human parts of the job can be humbling, grounding and uplifting in equal measure. Find your Dogdog.

My eldest daughter is somewhat of a shero. She is one of those children who whatever she touches she seems to be good at (except maybe tidying her room unlike her immaculate younger sister). She always excels in all subjects at school, is usually brilliantly behaved and is a hugely talented athlete. It is as though she has the Midas touch with everything she does, and my middle daughter adores her, as does my son. She is obsessed with football and knows every stat of every fixture, every player and every ground in the country. She adores maths and science and hates pink. She's pretty much dashing through life at 100mph and smashing every stereotype along the way. She is an insatiable reader and devours anything to do with Harry Potter or football and when she was younger she used to spend hours reading to her younger siblings for which I will be eternally grateful as it bought me a few precious moments to attend to the non-stop household carnage the three of them used to create daily. She would sit one of them either side of her, pick up a well-loved book and read to them, initially with the faltering early reading of her five-year-old self but later full of expression, questions about the characters and quiet reprimands for wriggling or page grabbing.

She was a joy to watch and she doesn't know but moments like this were utterly beautiful as I watched the three of them function as a little family trinity and I could see all the hours of reading and parenting I'd poured into my first being lived large again through her behaviour with her younger siblings. They both always want to play with her and as she gets older, the games she wants to play don't always dovetail with those of her younger siblings' requests, but nevertheless she often indulges them and plays along for a while and when she does, the house is often at its noisiest, its most fun and absolutely full of learning as she imparts her playing knowledge and life experience to her brother and sister. I have so many family photos of the three of them where I've tried desperately to get them all looking at the camera in the same way, but invariably one of them is just gazing in awe and wonder at my eldest.

They look to her for guidance on pretty much everything and when they're about to leap off the play equipment in the garden, have hurt themselves or need help with something, they often go to her before they come to me. So I've given up on trying to get them all facing the front on pictures and actually now love the ones where they are looking to her for guidance and support as it reminds me that this is something I need to continue to do in leadership. Just by chance, at each of my career stages, in all of my different roles, I have been lucky enough to work with at least one utterly stellar colleague. These are the kind of colleagues who are just unbelievably brilliant at their jobs, who not only do the basics brilliantly but who seem to tap into innovative or latest thinking about how to improve performance. Nobody seems even close to them in terms of talent, generosity of spirit and ability to build teams. I have been so fortunate in that in each workplace I've always had not just one but often two or more of these magic colleagues, and in the wider networks I've built across my sector, I'm now coming across more and more inspirational, collegiate and committed flashes of brilliance.

Just as my two younger siblings have been in awe of their eldest sister, so too have I been in awe of my colleagues along the way. It would have been really easy to watch their ways of working from afar and attempt to emulate them exactly, but that would have ended in disaster. When looking at unique brilliance that's exactly what it is – unique to them. Any attempt to directly replicate the approach of a colleague has you ending up looking like a bad tribute act on *Stars in Their Eyes* as you try to capture the way they walk, talk, interact and go about their business.

By working alongside them, asking them directly to support you in your own development, you are ensuring that you are sprinkled with their stardust. Just as my eldest would sit my two youngest down to share with them her skill of reading or playing, so too should we seek out someone to sit down and share a bit of wisdom with us. Whether we seek this formally by attending coaching or networking events, or whether we just ask a person whose work we admire if they could help us, we are all going to need someone to help us climb the rocky and potentially exhausting leadership mountain. Without someone, who at least knows one way up the face of it and who can support us, we will find this virtually impossible. Expecting to develop as a leader without the support of a network of existing specialists and experts is a little like expecting Neil Armstrong to have got himself onto the surface of the moon without NASA. Every leadership journey requires inspiration, innovation, energy, reflection *and* guidance. Although we have our own moral compass to help set the course for most decisions, we also need specialist guides and inspirational figures to fire continued aspirations and to give us a hand or catch us when we are about to fall off the leadership play equipment.

If you're in an organisation where stardust is slim pickings then the joy of social media and networking events mean that it is easier than ever to find and connect with people in the same field as you or whose work you admire. Long gone is the old-fashioned six degrees of separation thing where you may have to wait years in a career for a series of mutual introductions and attendance on courses to link you to a person you admire. Nowadays a single tweet or comment on other networking sites can take you directly to the people you want to speak to. I was reminded of the Victorian practice of calling cards and all the associated etiquette recently while absentmindedly Googling; I absolutely marvelled at the pages upon pages of etiquette and rules and the scandals that could be unleashed should one fail to adhere to the strict code. All of those regulations and societal rigmarole just to get to say hello to someone (and you wouldn't even be allowed to take your coat off apparently). I cannot imagine how long it would take to build up a professional network if those rules were still in place today.

Fortunately we have the whole world via the internet to call upon now and not just Victorian society with its dainty sandwiches and rules about where you can put your bonnet. We can tap into any sphere, any level of expertise or experience and begin to build vast networks at a pace the Victorians could only dream of, plus we can do it all in our pyjamas from the comfort of our own homes if we want to and no one is going to berate us for wearing a hat in the parlour or if we're attempting to make a call on a rainy day (apparently this was most ungracious). We can also take a leaf out of our toddler books in terms of making these types of connections too.

Toddlers have zero fear of hierarchies and social niceties. If anything, the more serious a situation and the more highly qualified or important the person in the room, the more likely our toddler is to do something utterly mortifying or – to coin a Victorian phrase – 'to display a lack of gentility or to display vulgarity'. I remember when we got married, my son, who was aged two at the time, spent most of the ceremony shouting about 'who's that man and what's he doing?' while pointing at the photographer. He then went on to accuse my mum of not reading him the storybook we had packed for him loudly enough (during the prayers), and then for a grand finale, threw up all over my wedding dress. They have no filter when it comes to making friends or interrupting conversations with the question you desperately wish they hadn't just asked. I've lost count of the number of times I've wanted the ground to open up and swallow me whole with their insightful but nevertheless cringingly bad questions. However I do admire their total lack of the stranglehold of politeness or being 'nice'. They connect with whomever they find interesting and always ask the question everyone is dying to ask but dare not.

Recently I've stopped trying to come across as if I'm always 100% competent and knowledgeable in all I do and have begun to actually enjoy asking what could be perceived as 'the stupid question'. Contrary to thinking the world would crumble and that there would be a collective sharp intake of breath, all eyes swivelling to burn into my incompetent forehead; what I actually see is more than likely a collective sigh of relief as everyone else can give up the charade of understanding what the hell is going on too. In leadership, I have found time after time there is an element of *The Emperor's New Clothes* in that everyone in a room maybe making what sounds like intellectual noises about a topic but if you actually admit you don't understand what's going on, you'll often find that there is at least one other person in the room who agrees with you that they haven't got a clue! The great thing about this is also that you are freed up from the guilt you may feel for not knowing or the pressure to cover up and carry on pretending that you do, but the real bonus is that if it does turn out you're the only one in the room who doesn't understand, do you know what you tend to get? Not gasps of horror but instead offers of help.

I can categorically say never have I been in a meeting whereupon admitting I've not understood something, I have received no offers of support to help get me up to speed. It's the quickest way to learn but one which so many of us are fearful of trying. I now have no qualms about asking questions or making connections with people. If my toddler can walk up to a stranger and make a friend immediately or can ask a question of someone they've never met and never be fazed then, at almost 40 years their senior, I should be able to too.

By doing exactly this I've met some of the most extraordinary people in the last 18 months. By simply asking them questions, attending events, lurching my way through social media and generally taking the stance of, 'oh well, what's the worst that could happen?' I've gone from a self-imposed endless Victorian etiquette gaol to a joyful gambol through a toddler-inspired meet and greet of brilliant people, all of whom have made me not only better at my job but have become my friends, confidantes, a supportive tribe and who (but they don't know it) make me look up to them and feel just like my youngest two do when they look at their elder sister.

Section 3:
To maternity and beyond!

Parenting, flexible working and leading differently

Chapter 1: The flexible leader

Maternity can be a lonely place. There, I've said it. Don't get me wrong, it's also a wonderful place and one I had struggled to get myself into for many years through many invasive hospital treatments and far too many tearful dashed hopes, but it's a lonely place nevertheless. For women who have lived and led wholeheartedly and devotedly in their day-to-day lives at work, the monotony and loneliness of being at home with a demanding baby in a new town in the middle of the harshest winter for decades, after a traumatic emergency delivery and with absolutely zero idea of how to look after a baby, believe me it can be incredibly lonely. And it is strange how you can feel so lonely when you are wanted all day, just as you were at work, only this time you receive no feedback other than tears or projectile vomit for quite a number of weeks so you don't even know if you're doing any of it right.

You adore your new 'colleague' and would go to the ends of the earth for them, but it is a strange feeling when where you really fancy going is not to the remote control for yet another episode of *Homes Under the Hammer*, or indeed to another baby class where you'll sit in a circle discussing intimate details of your birth with people whose names you don't even yet know, whilst waving a maraca and a chiffon scarf and singing *Wind the Bobbin Up*, but where you really fancy going is somewhere where you swore blind you wouldn't miss – work. Work with all its busyness, chaos, complicated thinking and close friendships with colleagues, and where you feel like you actually know what you're doing. Whilst on maternity leave – the three times I took it – I didn't miss the early morning commutes in standstill traffic, the endless meetings, the paperwork or the occasionally infuriating colleague, but what I missed was the camaraderie of the workplace and the feeling that your mind was being challenged and you had something to contribute other than milk and clean nappies.

My children are my absolute world but when you have studied and worked hard for decades in a job you love, parting can be a huge wrench, thus leaving behind a huge gap in your life and subsequently making you feel incredibly lonely. For many years I had been defined by my work. I had been Emma the teacher, Emma the consultant, Emma the school leader and I had been confident that I was pretty good at all those things. Now, in my new role, I wasn't so sure I was actually any good at my new job. Welcome then, a big round of applause for that most frequent of visitors during this huge life change – imposter syndrome. The sneaky will-o'-the-wisp that is imposter syndrome likes to nip in and out during maternity leave to ambush you when you least expect it. The thing is, when you're on maternity leave, imposter syndrome tends to bring his twin with him so they can tag team you with one sitting on your shoulder, whispering about what a rubbish parent you are, and the other on the other side telling you that you've lost your sparkle and credibility at work. They're not there all the time but they definitely like to pop in every now and again just to chip away at your confidence that is currently under reconstruction and being bulldozed to the ground along with rational thought by the absolute thundering swine that is sleep deprivation.

Being on maternity leave can be a glorious round of coffee dates with newfound friends, watching the joy of your baby grow and achieve new milestones, and the unbridled joy of bonding with your baby, but it can also be frustrating, bewildering and isolating. I remember I had to catch a bus to see my mum not long after my first C-section. My (now) husband worked away a lot during the week and so I was going to go to my mum and dad's to stay for a night or two. The bus left the end of my road at 11:30am in the morning, which is plenty of time for an educated, capable woman who can run an entire school to get herself and just one baby down the road with an overnight bag and on that bus, right? Wrong. At 11:25am I was on the phone to my mum sobbing that I couldn't seem to get my daughter out of the house. Every time I went to try and pick her up she would be sick or need changing or feeding, and I now had absolutely no clean bedding, towels or sheets left and the one pair of clean leggings which were the only thing that still fitted me had just been decorated with yet more baby sick. I look back now and laugh, especially as by baby number three and the same number of days postpartum I had got all three kids up, dressed, breakfasted, reading books done and all walked the mile to school well before 8:30am, but at the time, imposter syndrome and his twin must have been sitting there with buckets of popcorn positively rolling in the aisles at the hilarity of it all. This highly qualified and successful leader of a school of 300+ pupils and dozens of staff can't even get herself dressed and out of the door by almost lunchtime without having to ring her mum.

Scenes like this were pretty common in the early days. I remember looking through the window of a coffee shop at other mums who were chatting happily whilst their babies cooed in prams next to them, whilst I had my unmade face pressed to the glass like Tiny Tim Cratchit marvelling at the myriad wonders within. It is hard to explain how much parenthood can wrong foot even the most confident of people. The huge physical, emotional and hormonal changes are recipe enough for self doubt to set in, but add in sleep deprivation and then a feeling that because you were a successful leader at work you should somehow be able to transfer this success to parenting, and then it all being a rather rude awakening, is a perfect storm for that nagging feeling of – as the song goes – 'things ain't what they used to be'.

My experience was shared by many of the first time mums I met in my local baby groups and thank god it was. Being able to share the joys and the horror stories we were all currently navigating was one of props that kept me going and helped maintain a sense of perspective about it all. And these feelings are not the sole preserve of those on maternity leave. Any large major life change can leave us feeling adrift and unsure and wondering if we'll ever regain our stardust. Moving house, dealing with serious illness or injury, caring for a spouse or elderly parents, all chip away at our confidence and our self belief. However pragmatically or positively you approach these situations they will always be a pull on your own feelings of capability. If you're unsure as to whether I'm right, consider this: when a colleague is feeling unsure of themselves or is looking for advice as to how to lighten their emotional or mental load, we always prescribe exercise, time with friends, more sleep or a holiday as balm for a bruised soul. We simply don't say, 'What you need to feel better is to relocate to a new area; your spouse to have an extended complicated stay in hospital; you to become sole carer for your elderly relatives and maybe chuck a baby or two into the mix.' We need to recognise as a profession that our colleagues are humans first, leaders second, and that changes at home have huge implications for people's ability and willingness to see themselves as a potential leader. Often these life changes come just at the point of career progression opportunity too, contributing to the ever-dwindling pool of people who want to step up and see themselves as a new leader. It is hard for many people to contemplate taking on yet more at work when their home lives are either chaotic, draining or in a state of flux. However, leadership is immensely doable and is often far more flexible and less draining than the day-to-day work in a non-leadership role.

One of the huge things I learnt as a leader with a young family was that, unlike when I was teaching, there were many aspects of leadership that were actually much easier than my teaching role. I didn't need to be in ridiculously early *every* morning as I wasn't shackled to the timetable of teaching lessons and so I didn't need to be in every single day to prep and be ready to teach. That's not to say I was slacking, but what slack it did provide was the opportunity to have a slightly later and less frenetic start on some (not all) days by scheduling a meeting to start at nine in the morning whereas when I was teaching, I would have needed to be in my classroom all set up by 8:20am. Coming in slightly later also meant that staff didn't feel as though they had to check in with me prior to their working day which was, although a lovely chance to catch up and check in, was not always the most productive use of their time.

Coming in with enough time to tackle any issues before the start of the day's core business, but not so early as to be constantly there with the lark was a revelation. This flexibility also meant that I could work later and without distraction some nights as rather than the face-to-face teaching commitments during the day, I could complete some of my work at other times. This was an aspect of leadership I'd totally overlooked. No one had ever explained to me that leadership is massively elastic and can be flexed much more easily than classroom teaching. Yes, I needed to be there early and stay late regularly for various commitments, but it also meant I didn't always need to be tearing into the car park in a huge panic. The pace of leadership was also a surprise. I had envisaged leadership to be a non-stop whirlwind of decision-making, meetings, a packed diary and far more work than my deputy role. I couldn't have been more wrong.

Yes, it was manic, yes it was frenetic but there was also a lot more reflection time and 'spare' time in which to catch up with tasks or to simply walk around the school and get involved with the day-to-day life of the organisation. The fact I no longer had a class but everyone else was busy teaching meant that there were these magical parts of the day where it was relatively quiet and therefore there was much more of an ebb and flow to the day. When I was juggling leadership and class teaching commitment this rhythm was far more staccato and frantic as I attempted to squeeze everything in. The luxury of a more steadily paced day was a previously hidden delight of leadership. This was a massive eye-opener for me and took me a lot of time to get used to. Yes it was busy and of course the accountability was often rather terrifying, as well as the initial learning curve, but the change of pace and the ability to actually go to the toilet when I needed to go – rather than waiting for breaks in between lessons – was pure joy! It is these aspects of leadership that need demystifying and discussing (but maybe not the toilet). There is so much out there about leadership traits and leadership behaviours and what you need to amass or acquire in terms of knowledge or skills, but rarely do people talk about the reality of leadership and the real benefits it can offer to those ready to take on a new challenge.

Leadership also comes with much more autonomy and that feeling of not constantly having to do things in a way that has been designed by somebody else, or to meet anyone's expectations other than your own, which can be massively liberating and helpful in terms of flexing your work. When no one is going to berate you for not having finished something or you are behind on a deadline and you realise the only person scheduling that deadline is you then that's a great feeling. Yes, of course, there are lines of accountability in any leadership role and especially in schools there are people more senior than the headteacher in the wider education organisational infrastructure, but there is significantly more autonomy in terms of workload and timetabling the completion of that work in a leadership role than there is in a classroom teacher role.

Despite completing my NPQH qualification, attending numerous leadership events and reading scores of leadership articles and books, no one had ever pointed any of this out and it was only once in the role where I realised that actually, sitting in the 'big chair' is a lot more accommodating and can actually make life a lot more comfortable! More autonomy is also great for confidence. It is well known and accepted that a feeling of a lack of autonomy is not good for mental health and wellbeing. Being in a leadership role where you can help set and chart the course, rather than being blown by the winds of another's whim, is a huge wallop for our old friend imposter syndrome, as well as helping to develop confidence in yourself as a leader.

Recently, I gave a presentation about the contents of this book and I spoke about the 'four horsemen of the leadership apocalypse', which sounds terribly dramatic but was only really used to act as a contrast for the last screen of the presentation I shared which I'll explain later. The four horsemen were as follows:

- Imposter syndrome
- Historical narrative about leadership styles
- Scale of emotional, physical, time resource, number of changes during parenthood
- Unspoken bias, weight of perceived judgement or pressure

The first one we have addressed already, but the second was not so much about what is typically said about leadership but what is simply implied. No leadership books discuss part-time leadership. No leadership books mention juggling work or family commitments, no leadership books discuss imposter syndrome or simply not feeling you are up to the job. It is almost as if once you enter the hallowed halls of leadership, you must shed your mortal skin and become an untouchable and committed superhuman who shall not be distracted by the call from nursery to say the baby has a temperature or from the care assistant who has found your mum has had a fall again. Nowhere I looked could I find anything that discussed the need to recognise and address the issue of 'feeling' like a leader or being a leader who might just have other pulls on their time or energy. It is this lack of discussion that can lead to the silent but deadly sub-narrative that leadership is not for the many but just the chosen committed few. And there are so many great but untapped leaders out there: so many people who are hearing the historical narrative and its associated whispery sub-narrative and thinking that leadership is terribly complicated and not for them. Believe me, it's tricky, tiring and a proper rollercoaster, but know this: no day in leadership is as bad as the day your toddler pukes in the ball pit at soft play, and I speak from experience.

We have touched on the scale of change in life that can affect your ability to see yourself as a leader, but we must also recognise as leaders (or potential leaders) that not only are we affected by these but so too are our colleagues. I have worked in schools before where staff were frightened to admit they were pregnant as they were unsure of their boss' response. I have also worked in schools where people were not allowed time off to attend the funeral of a dear friend because it didn't fit exactly with the school's leave policy. These are sadly not uncommon and are part of the reason we need to encourage the widest range of people possible into leadership roles. Life experience makes us compassionate and understanding leaders with a heightened awareness of the need to look after staff and create a culture of openness and support in the workplace. My former co-head colleague and I managed to have five babies in five years during the time we worked in this setup and did everything from hook ourselves up to breast pumps, whilst on the phone to the Department for Education, to bringing babies into meetings when there were childcare emergencies. We sought parenting advice from seasoned parents and grandparents on the staff and I remember once feeling so broken by sleep deprivation and exhaustion that I was stumbling over the making of an early morning cup of tea. One of our teachers (a mum and grandma herself) gave me a huge hug in an empty staffroom as I snivelled next to the tea urn; I will never forget her kindness in that moment and her perceptive observation of my quiet struggle.

This kind of honesty helped to set the tone and culture for the school where it was clear that we were all humans first, leaders and teachers second. Subsequently, this led to high rates of retention as staff felt valued and cared for. Seeing us both doing leadership differently and navigating the tricky trials of new parenting and leadership meant that we were unknowingly demystifying leadership for anyone watching. Becoming a parent whilst in a leadership role also made me efficient in terms of completing work that needed to be done. Whereas before I may have tinkered with a project or faffed about with a layout or overthought a conversation, I now simply didn't have the time to stew or to overthink. The mantra of 'done is better than perfect' was another revelation and actually meant that in meetings conversations about a draft document or an unfinished piece of thinking were far more productive as colleagues genuinely now felt they were contributing and being consulted, rather than just being handed another fait accompli. This is not to say that, by contrast, being a perfectionist makes you a bad leader, or indeed that leaders who don't have huge swathes of life experience are all hateful tyrants devoid of a single compassionate bone in their bodies, but instead that leadership is multi-faceted and hugely diverse.

If we think of the thousands of types of organisations needing to be led and the myriad of different combinations of skills and expertise each one requires, then a one size fits all model of leadership and its associated narrow singular narratives is simply not going to work. As a profession and as future leaders we need to recognise that for every pot there's a lid and that our own skills, experience and knowledge fingerprint is the perfect match for an organisation out there.

There is also the weight of perceived judgement out there about work and life commitments. In regard to parenting there is the ever-present dichotomy of being required to work as if you don't have children but parent as if you don't work. Even if this culture is not present in your workplace, or is one to which you subscribe yourself, it is nevertheless hanging in the air like a cloying mist in many other environments. It was clear after a while in a part time leadership role and as a parent of three small children that I was always going to be wrong. If I worked full time I'd be criticised for leaving my children in full time childcare. If I gave up work, I'd be a statistic. If I worked part time in leadership I'd be met regularly with raised eyebrows and a healthy dose of cynicism and scepticism as to how exactly that worked and how effective it could possibly be. Sadly it is still all too often women who have the bear the brunt of these types of judgements. It is still rare for anyone to enquire as to a father's working plans after children arrive on the scene and I am yet to hear a father criticised for not staying at home with his children and instead going out to work full time.

The reasoning behind this is immensely complex and is explored in many books and research, but it is important to recognise that this existing weight of perceived or actual judgement as to whether or not to pursue leadership following the arrival of children is yet another burden many new mothers feel they have to carry. A father who receives a promotion shortly after a baby arrives would be congratulated. By contrast, a woman who pursued a promotion in the same way would undoubtedly receive much more mixed responses to her workplace success. Thankfully the narrative around the motherhood penalty is becoming better known, but its pervasive and lingering text does still loom large on the leadership horizon for many new mothers. It is this same perceived judgement that can mean people who have other commitments or who have chronic conditions themselves may feel unable to disclose their own circumstances for fear or judgement, or who may feel that they are not able to pursue leadership as they have pulls on their time and energy.

Leadership, in a similar way to the traditional marriage vows, should not be entered into lightly but reverently and wholeheartedly, and much like the marriage vows it should also include the aspects of 'for richer for poorer, in sickness and in health'. If we are to be wedded to our jobs and our leadership positions in terms of the time we commit and energy we devote then we also need them to be accommodating of our own life challenges and not divorce ourselves from the prospect of leadership simply because of our lives outside work. Leadership is not the preserve of those in the first flushes of youthful optimism, energy and a love of the job but also, just like marriage, is an institution into which anyone can legally enter, therefore the prospect of entering the leadership of an institution should be as welcoming and supportive and as fulfilling a relationship.

My final screen in the presentation was a contrast to the four horsemen, and in line with the lighthearted and informal structure of the event where I presented, was entitled: 'The joyful unicorn of leadership development'. The deliberate use of a mystical creature served the purpose of emphasising that leadership needs to actually be demystified to encourage a wider range of people into leadership, and to point out that it is one of the most joyful jobs you can do. This raised a smile and a laugh from the assembled attendees but the point I wanted to make was anything but light hearted.

The slide contained the following 4 points:
• Leadership is more flexible
• Leadership enables greater autonomy – autonomy develops confidence
• Leadership needs demystifying
• Leadership evolving – natural maturation

The final point was one which still requires much work, both in terms of the way we talk about leadership and its associated behaviours, but also in terms of what we expect from our leadership structures and systems. The world outside teaching has offered flexible working for some time, but education is slow to catch up. There have been job shares in class teacher roles for many years but within leadership this is a much slower pace of change. There is beginning to be movement and it is gathering pace but the one leader, one role, one school model is still very much in the majority. It is also embedded in the psyche and experience of pretty much every adult who has been a pupil in our education system.

The historical narrative around leadership is very much coloured by our own and our peers' experience of education leaders as being a sole figure who worked full time. Part time is of course only an option. Many leaders who don't currently see themselves as leaders would ideally like to work full time, but the point is that the system is slow to embrace both sorts of change: those leaders who want to work part time and those leaders who want to lead in a different style. Both will encounter obstacles along the way both in terms of ingrained models, unconscious bias or just fear of the unknown. What we need to do to demystify leadership is to pull the curtain from in front of the leadership conjurer's table and reveal that effective leadership is not actually magic. We need to present alternative views and narratives around effective leadership and begin to articulate the simple truths around successful leadership behaviours and also make leadership attractive for those who may currently be in awe of the leadership magicians.

Chapter 2: The future of leadership

When I reflect on my own experience of leadership, I find that it was a bit of a wonky one in that I've done leadership at a young age, part time leadership in a job share, leadership during maternity, and part time leadership without a job share. It seems simple to me that leadership isn't a one size fits all. However, I am all too aware that the path I trod was very much an unknown one in many respects. Throughout every step though I had people who believed in me, maverick champions who said, 'why not?' and 'let's just do it anyway' or 'what's the worst that could happen?'. And so far, it's all kind of worked out OK!

Now imposter syndrome would have me say that this was just luck or fluke, and I often wonder if this was and still is. However, there's another school of thought that says you make your own luck, and also if a system accommodates change then it's ready for change. There is a crisis in recruitment and retention across all aspects of education. Budgets are being slashed and teachers and leaders are leaving in droves. Subsequently, there will be an imminent gaping black hole in the leadership recruitment universe and so something out of the ordinary will have to happen in order to fill these gaps. This is where the perceived fading or currently hidden stardust of so many that don't currently see themselves as leaders needs to start shining. When I talk to the hundreds of people I meet on conferences, at events and online, so many say they could never see themselves as a leader, and yet they are leading aspects of their lives and classrooms with such grace, competence and aplomb they are already modelling honed and highly-skilled leadership behaviours.

Every teacher who successfully manages a class, writes a curriculum and manages the behaviour of 30 young people every day, day in day out, as well as navigating relationships with parents, support assistants and the wider staff, is already a master at leadership. What we often fail to do as teachers and as people is to recognise that our skills are ultimately transferrable and that a lot of leadership is ultimately just as much about being genuine, honest and human as it is about knowledge and experience. I have met hundreds of headteachers over the years and one of my first ever thoughts when walking into a room of these revered folk as a newly appointed head was that they looked so normal and no different or any more skilled necessarily than I could become or was. The most demystifying part of leadership for me was being in a room with loads of other leaders and realising that away from the names on their doors, whilst chatting over coffee and registration at an event, they were simply everyday people. What I also noticed is that every headteacher I've ever met has been brilliant at some things and then conversely has an Achilles heel. For some they are great orators and team builders but hopelessly disorganised. For others they are frighteningly knowledgeable but terrified by public speaking. For others they run a really tight ship in terms of budget and systems but they appear aloof or rely on others in their organisation to boost morale and wellbeing. Each has their individual talents and each has their foibles and absolutely none are the finished article. En masse they would be a force to be reckoned with as they would have all the bases covered, but individually they are as fallible and nuanced as anyone else.

Recognising that we already have and regularly employ leadership behaviours is the first step to seeing ourselves as leader. Recognising then that we don't have to be perfect at all aspects of leadership is the next. Within any new role we take on we will grow and develop, as we experience the new challenges and demands of the job. For too many a leadership job description is a set of ingredients for a single recipe where should one ingredient be missing it would cause the entire dish to collapse and be utterly inedible. For others, seeing that leadership job description is a list of ingredients, some of which they may not currently have but what they do possess is the vision to see what exactly can be created with the ingredients they *do* currently have. Leadership roles are not a grand and final destination led to by a careful treading of an exact route but a place in which we can arrive in a myriad of ways and continue to learn. The day we think we know everything there is to know about leadership is the day we probably need to leave. What leadership needs is integrity, ingenuity, intelligence, honesty, insight and bravery, however these are not amassed necessarily through courses or standardised routes and programmes.

I entered leadership myself on purpose and quite by accident too, but each time the associated leadership learning and behaviours I developed would all later be echoed through those of my toddlers. My first leadership role began in university when, realising there was some dissatisfaction with the organisation of the course content and structure amongst my course peers, I approached the head of the course to share my views. They asked me then if I would become a student representative for the course and to help them resolve any existing or future issues. This led to me meeting regularly with senior university staff to review the course and to share feedback between staff and students. It was a role I didn't initially relish: the pull of the student union was very strong, but I felt I had a moral duty to ensure that this was put right, not just for me but for all of the other student teachers and subsequently the children they would be teaching. It was my first brush with feeling a sense of righteous indignation and moral purpose – this was my chocolate buttons moment for the first time.

After joining my first school as a newly qualified teacher I was lucky enough to work alongside some of the most talented and knowledgeable teachers I have met in 22 years of teaching. I was hungry to learn from them and constantly badgered them for feedback, advice and opportunities to shadow them. I must have been like some kind of annoying mosquito, but I so wanted to get things right for the children in my class that I knew I had to keep on learning and developing from those who had so obviously just got it right. This is something I have continued to do throughout my career although hopefully with less of a resemblance to a pesky insect. Learning from people who inspire you is key to moving on, as is having the good grace to admit that you definitely don't know everything and being prepared to be vulnerable and admit that you need help.

As a consultant for a national strategy I was able to visit scores of different schools and began to hone my own views of what I truly believed in. Through observing hundreds of different staff, leaders and systems I learnt so much about not only what I would do if I were ever to be a school leader but also what I wouldn't do and what I'd say no to every time. This role also taught me about the power of collegiality and networking. The friendships and connections I made throughout this time meant I had a wide and experienced network to call upon when I did find myself in a leadership position. If you were thinking of leadership, one big piece of advice I would give anyone would be to widen your networks, and then when you think they're wide, widen them even more. Almost 20 years on, I still run into people I met during this role and call upon the skills and expertise of so many of them in my day-to-day work.

Through working as a co-headteacher I learnt the true value of support and collegiality and the power of doing something differently. You may have no points of reference or blueprints, but there is nothing more joyously terrifying and exhilarating than breaking the mould, smashing stereotypes and throwing yourself wholeheartedly into something you believe in.

In my current role I am lucky enough to have the time to constantly read, research, learn and develop. I devour books and articles as well as relish in the learning points I glean from training events and networking. Through writing and delivering hundreds of CPD sessions I'm able to hear stories from all aspects of the sector and all career stages; this constant learning, investigation and making of new friends and connections means that I'm constantly developing new skills, amassing professional knowledge, questioning and taking on new challenges. Every day is a new day in my role and the chance to build new teams, try new things and learn from some of my edu-superheroes; it also means that, just like my toddlers, I'm constantly learning whilst calling on the skills of those more experienced or knowledgeable than me. If you had asked me at the start of my career whether leadership is something that I aspired after, I would have probably shied away from it. However, leadership has provided me not only with constant interest, challenge and often hilarity but also brought me balance in my life, confidence and a real feeling of accomplishment. Leadership is definitely not just for a select few or a narrow section of the population. There is leadership potential in so many of us. So, find your chocolate buttons, be resolute in your celery and become that joyous unicorn of leadership development. Put simply,

Be More Toddler.

CPSIA information can be obtained
at www.ICGtesting.com
Printed in the USA
LVHW041530191219
641071LV00003B/4/P

9 781912 906727